Tax Planning For Company Owners

Lee Hadnum LLB ACA CTA

WPR Tax Publishing

Important Legal Notices

Tax Planning For Company Owners

Published by:

WPR Tax Publishing
BCB Bachstrasse 1
CH-9606 Butschwil
Switzerland

email: sales@wealthprotectionreport.co.uk

2nd Edition, April 2013

ISBN 978-0-9576024-2-7

Disclaimer
Before reading or relying on the content of this guide, please read the disclaimer carefully.

Disclaimer

1. Please note that this tax guide is intended as **general guidance only** for individual readers and does NOT constitute accountancy, tax, legal, investment or other professional advice. WealthProtectionReport and the author accept no responsibility or liability for loss which may arise from reliance on information contained in this tax guide.

2. Please note that tax legislation, the law and practices by government and regulatory authorities (for example, HM Revenue and Customs) are constantly changing and the information contained in this tax guide is only correct as at the date of publication. We therefore recommend that for accountancy, tax, investment or other professional advice, you consult a suitably qualified accountant, tax specialist, independent financial adviser, or other professional adviser. Please also note that your personal circumstances may vary from the general examples given in this tax guide and your professional adviser will be able to give specific advice based on your personal circumstances.

3. This tax guide covers UK taxation mainly and any references to 'tax' or 'taxation' in this tax guide, unless the contrary is expressly stated, are to UK taxation only. Please note that references to the 'UK' do not include the Channel Islands or the Isle of Man. Addressing all foreign tax implications is beyond the scope of this tax guide.

4. Whilst in an effort to be helpful, this tax guide may refer to general guidance on matters other than UK taxation, WealthProtectionReport and the author are not experts in these matters and do not accept any responsibility or liability for loss which may arise from reliance on such information contained in this tax guide.

Contents

Chapter 1

Introduction

Using a UK company can be very attractive for a number of reasons. Crucially though:

- It is classed as a separate legal entity and can sue and be sued in its own name. It can therefore be useful for asset protection purposes and

- It is subject to much lower rates of tax than an individual.

The highest rate of personal income tax is 45% from April 2013. However the highest headline rate of tax a company pays is 23% (from April 2013).

This can represent a significant benefit, particularly where business owners retain profits within the company.

The Government is keen to reduce the rates of corporation tax, particularly the main rate of corporation tax payable by large companies (i.e. usually companies that make more than £1.5M in profit per year – unless there are associated companies). This is being reduced to 21% from April 2014 and 20% from April 2015.

It's not just the largest companies that benefit though. Companies that make profits above £300,000, pay their tax partly at the lower rate and partly at the higher rate, so they also benefit. The effective rate of tax payable on profits within the "marginal rate band" (£300,000 - £1.5M if you own just one company) has reduced from 25% in 2012 and will be just 23.75% after April 2013.

Even though the tax rates are reducing, company owners will still be looking at opportunities to further reduce the company and personal taxes they will be liable to.

In this book, we look at a variety of different aspects of tax planning for companies and company owners.

Chapter 2

Why Use A Company?

In this chapter, we will recap on the main reason for using a company.

The main benefit in using a company is that it is taxed separately from you as an individual.

Therefore if you traded in your own name you would be taxed at 20%, 40% or 45% depending on the level of the profits/your income.

If you trade as a Limited company the company will pay tax at the main rates of either 20% or 23%. For anyone with income/profits above the higher rate tax band there can therefore be significant advantages to using a company. The level of corporation tax will be significantly less than the level of income tax if they traded in their own name.

Of course this isn't the end of the matter. There is also income tax to take into account when the shareholders extract profits from the company. This is now usually structured as dividends as dividends now result in a larger take home pay then a salary payment.

The income tax charge on the extraction of funds from the company significantly reduces the tax attractiveness of using a company, particularly where all of the profits are extracted. The tax rates on dividends (25% for higher rate taxpayers and 30.55% for additional rate taxpayers) as well as the corporation tax charges pretty much eliminate the tax benefit of the lower rates of corporation tax.

However, where profits are retained in the company – or at least some of the profits are retained in the company, there can still be significant advantages to using a company.

This is the main reason for using a company: The ability to reinvest profits allows for a deferral of the tax payable.

Of course if the profits are extracted in the future there would then be income tax payable, but you could look to extracting free of tax as a non-resident or liquidating the company and extracting as a capital distribution (potentially paying just 10% CGT).

Chapter 3

Should You Even Be Using A Company?

Much has been written on when you should use a UK company. As we've seen above, the ability to reinvest profits can lead to a significant reduction in the total tax payable. However, this is not always the case. There are occasions when using a UK company can actually increase the amount of tax payable.

We've listed some of the main occasions below:

Where the company would be classed as a close investment company ('CIC')

The tax legislation states that a close company is a CIC unless throughout the accounting period it exists wholly or mainly for one or more of the following purposes:

a) The purpose of carrying on a trade or trades on a commercial basis

b) The purpose of making investments in land or estates or interests in land in cases where the land is, or is intended to be, let to persons other than

i) Any person connected with the relevant company, or
ii)Any person who is the wife or husband of an individual connected with the relevant company, or is a relative, or the wife or husband of a relative, of such an individual or of the husband or wife of such an individual

Therefore if you are using a company as a non property investment company the chances are you will be caught by these provisions. This would include holding an intangible asset or investing in shares via a company.

Investments in land have a specific let out in that providing the property is let to an unconnected party the company would not be a CIC. If though you used a separate property company to hold property that was let to your trading company you could easily fall within the CIC rules.

Where the CIC rules apply the company is charged at 23% irrespective of the level of profits.

When you consider that this is just the company's tax charge and that an additional tax charge would arise on the shareholders/directors on the extraction of funds (potentially at 25% for a higher rate taxpayer extracting dividends rising to 30.55% for someone with income above £150,000) you could easily end up paying more tax by using a company than if you invested personally.

When you also add into the equation the fact that individuals would usually be entitled to higher reliefs on disposals of capital assets (e.g., the annual exemption) and would be taxed at 28% (and just 18% within their basic rate band) this swings the balance even more in favour of personal investment.

If you are planning on going overseas

This is something that many people overlook, but given the number of people emigrating and working from overseas (e.g. telecommuting) it's well worth bearing in mind.

Imagine this. You write a few e-books and decide to sell them over the internet. Since you live in the UK, you know all about the advantages of a UK company; therefore, you transfer the rights to the books over to the company at start up and trade via the UK company.

Five years later, the company has become profitable, and generates royalties of £75,000 per annum. You have got sick of life in the UK and want to move to Cyprus.

There is no problem with you personally moving to Cyprus; the downside is that the e-books are locked in the UK company. Any transfer of the e-books out of the UK company would crystallise a gain in the UK company, based on the market value of the books (likely to be substantial if they're generating £75,000 pa) and the original acquisition cost (nominal).

Therefore, the fact that you never set foot in the UK, would not stop the UK taxman taking 20% of the profits of the UK royalty company. There would also be a risk that if you stopped trading from the company after leaving the UK (to prevent other income being taxed in the UK), that the UK taxman could class the company as a CIC, and thus, tax it at 23%.

The fact that Cyprus is generally regarded as a royalty tax haven would not matter to you as you would not be able to take advantage of it,at least not without incurring a hefty tax cost.

The other downside of retaining a UK company is that you can not completely sever your ties with the UK, as you will still be in receipt of UK dividends. You could incorporate an overseas company to hold the shares but this is 'messy' and could anyway lead to an increase in the number of associated companies/tax rate dependent on what the holding company does.

If you are trading personally you won't have any of these problems. There is no deemed disposal of assets when you cease to be UK resident (unlike in many countries) and you could just carry out the trade from overseas. Provided you have no UK trade there will then be no UK tax charges.

Occupying property

If you are looking at purchasing property which you will or even may occupy this should not be owned by a company.

The use of a company in this case has a number of disadvantages including:

- The fact that the property will be locked in the company. Any disposal of the property would crystallise a gain in the company (subject to corporation tax) as well as a further tax charge on the extraction of the proceeds

- The reliefs available to a company are much less than an individual. In particular if you have occupied the property as your main residence you would qualify for principal private residence ('PPR') relief on a disposal. In addition the annual exemption would be due. This will in many cases fully eliminate any gain.

By contrast a company would not be entitled to any of these reliefs and would be fully charged to corporation tax on the gain with only a small amount of relief for the effects of inflation.

- Any occupation of the property by you without you paying the company a market rental would be classed as a benefit in kind from the company to you. The broad effect of this is that you are likely to be subject to an annual income tax charge on approximately the market rental income the company could have obtained.

Therefore owning a personal residence via a company is obviously a big "no no."

If you are a non UK domiciliary

If you are a non UK domiciliary you are generally taxed on overseas income and gains to the extent that the income or proceeds are remitted to the UK (i.e. brought into the UK) if you make the claim.

In this case, if you own overseas assets or are conducting a trade overseas, using a UK company may not be advisable. A UK company would usually be classed as resident in the UK, and as such would be subject to corporation tax on its worldwide income and gains.

Given as a non UK domiciliary you could own personally and avoid UK tax by retaining income or gains overseas using a UK company would not be advisable (providing you could retain some of the cash overseas).

Incorporation followed by a quick sale

Transferring your business to a company could be disastrous if you are then made an offer you cannot refuse for the shares.

As the owner of the unincorporated business, you could probably sell benefiting from Entreprencurs relief (i.e. the 10% rate of CGT on gains of up to £10,000,000). When you transfer the business to the company, you then own the shares and a new period of ownership begins. A disposal of the shares within twelve months of the share acquisition would not entitle you to any Entrepreneurs relief.

Even if you incorporated the company years before and left it dormant, you would not have more than one year qualifying ownership because the company would only be a trading company when the trade was transferred into it.

Assets held long term

If you are holding property or assets long term for investment potential buy holding via a company, the company loses out on the 28% rate of capital gains tax.

The company would only get meagre indexation relief with any gains then subject to corporation tax at 20-23% and a further income tax charge (likely to be at 25% or 30.55%) on the extraction of profits.

You could always sell the shares in the company instead of the company selling the assets. You would then qualify for the 18%/28% rate of CGT on gains within your basic rate band and also potentially Entrepreneurs Relief. The downside to this is that any purchaser is very likely to look for a discount in the value of the company to reflect the fact that the company has an unrealised tax liability. This means you will not get anywhere near as much for the shares as you would if you sold the assets personally.

If you cannot retain profits in the company

The benefit of the company is that it has a lower rate of tax than you do personally. If you extract cash from the company you then incur a personal tax charge which eliminates much of the benefit of using the company.

So, if you hold personally you may suffer a 40% or 45% tax charge (as well as NI if you are a trader). If you hold via a company, the company may suffer a tax charge of 20% (if profits are less than £300,000), and you would suffer an effective tax rate at 25% on extraction of dividends.

When you take into account the other drawbacks of using a company, including the higher accounting and filing fees, extra admin etc., the benefits may not be worthwhile.

If you need to make significant pension contributions

You may find it better to trade personally if you need to make large pension contributions.

Your ability to make pension contributions and get tax relief on them now depends on the level of your earned income. Therefore, if you are trading personally, you could potentially make a pension contribution of the amount of your net profit, (subject to the usual rules regarding the annual and lifetime pension limits). You would be taxed at 40%/45%, but the pension would qualify for tax relief.

If you use a company, the company would be taxed on the profits generated. In order to make a large pension contribution, you would need to have significant earned income.

Dividend income is not classed as earned income, and therefore, you would need to extract cash as salary/bonus to use this as a 'base' for your pension contribution. The downside to this is that NIC charges would result (although only at 2% above the upper earnings limit) and on the company.

The company would pay NIC at 13.8% on the full amount of the bonus, although it would be tax deductible.

In this case, the salary payment could in itself reduce the benefit of using a company significantly. The company may still have the edge, but it would be more marginal, and when you take other issues into account... well that's up to you.

Chapter 4

How to Extend the £300,000 Small Company Band & Avoid the 23% CT Rate

The effective rates of corporation tax from April 2013 are:

0-300,000=	20%
£300,000-1.5M=	23.75%
£1.5M+=	23%

So, if your business earned more than £300,000 you would not be subject to the 20% rate of corporation tax anymore but would instead be taxed at 23.75% on profits above £300,000.

Once your profits exceed £300,000, you will see your corporation tax rate jump up immediately.

You cannot avoid these rules by simply setting up another company to carry out some of the trading and splitting the profits between the two (to keep below the £300,000 limit), as the associated company provisions would then apply.

The associated company provisions would result in the tax bands available to each company being halved (if there was one associated company).

How can the small company band be extended to larger profits?

One option to avoid the increased rates of corporation tax would be to use a partnership or LLP to carry out part of the trade. As these are not subject to the associated company rules, the profits would be split between the company and the partnership. The former would be subject to corporation tax at 20% if profits were less than £300,000. In terms of the partnership though, this would be subject to income tax.

If you wanted to avoid income tax completely and have all of the profits subject to the small company rates of corporation tax, you could consider using a corporate partnership.

In this case, you would have company A and company B in a partnership carrying out the trade.

The profits of the partnership would be allocated to A and B in accordance with the agreed profit sharing ratio. So, if profits were £500,000, for instance with a 50/50 profit sharing ratio, each company would be taxed at 20%. The total corporation tax would be £100,000.

If you used a single company which generated profits of £500,000, the corporation tax liability would be £107,500. The tax saving would, therefore, be £7,500.

You could potentially use this strategy to have even larger partnerships which could even avoid the 23% rate of corporation tax.

Points to watch out for

There is one key issue that would need to be considered before this strategy would be successful:

Firstly, you would need to ensure that the two companies were not associated with each other. The tax legislation will class a company as an associated company of another at any given time when:

- one of the companies has control of the other, or
- both of the companies are under the control of the same person or persons.

You would therefore need to avoid this second requirement and ensure that both of the companies are not under the control of the same person or persons. HMRC will only regard the two companies as under the control of the same persons if:

- a group which controls one company is identical with a group which controls the other, and
- for each company, that group is a 'minimum controlling combination'.

A 'minimum controlling combination' means a group of persons that has control of the company but which would not have control of it if any one of the persons were excluded from the group.

Essentially, you would need to look at the individuals who control Company A and see if any of those individuals either on their own or in combination can also control Company B.

'Great' you think, "I'll set up both companies with different directors and shareholders."

But, in addition to the rights and powers which an individual has, the rights and powers of certain other people may be attributed to him and count as his rights for the purpose of determining who controls the company.

Crucially, the rights and powers of his associates are taken into account.

What is an associate?

An associate of a participator is:

a. a person in any of the following relationships to the participator:

i) husband or wife,
ii) parent or remoter forebear,
iii) child or remoter issue,

iv) brother or sister,
v) partner.

Separated spouses are regarded as associated with each other, but divorced spouses are not. Other relatives are regarded as associated only if there is a blood relationship. E.g.,, half-sisters are associated, but stepsisters are not).

What does this mean?

Look at the people who control the companies you need to ensure.Your associated people should not be controlling the two companies. If you did, the two companies themselves would be associated and the tax bands would be split if there was substantial commercial interdependence between the two companies. If there was not any "substantial commercial interdependence" between the two companies, then after April 2011 the companies would not be connected.

Substantial commercial interdependence may exist, for example, if the companies share staff, premises and equipment, cooperate on projects or have substantial dealings with each other.

Exception for Unmarried Couples

Lots of couples are not legally married but raise children, start businesses and buy property together.

However, unmarried couples are not recognised by the tax system (with one or two exceptions, e.g. tax credits). In many cases, this is a drawback, but it is a big advantage when it comes to running multiple companies.

An unmarried couple can each set up a uniquely owned company and can benefit from up to £600,000 of profits taxed at 20%, even if there is substantial commercial interdependence between the two companies.

(Note, that if an unmarried couple have a separate partnership business, they would also be business partners, and the associated company rules would apply.)

Companies with Identical Shareholdings

If you form two or more companies with the same shareholdings ,they will continue to be associated, even if there is not substantial commercial interdependence between them.

Example

Sarah and her husband John each own 50% of Company A.

They also each own 50% of Company B.

There is no commercial connection between the two companies, but they are associated companies because they are controlled by the same persons.

However, if Sarah transfers 1% or more of Company A to John and John transfers 1% or more of company B to Sarah, they will each control one of the companies - the companies will no longer be controlled by the same people and will not be associated.

Tax Planning Pointers - Associated Companies

- If neither your existing company, nor your new venture, is likely to make profits over £150,000, you may not have to worry about setting up a second company.

- If setting up a new company will result in a higher tax bill, consider running your new business venture out of the same company or as a sole trader or partnership.

- Limited liability for the new venture can be preserved without affecting your existing company's corporation tax bill by using a limited liability partnership (LLP).

- Where a new venture may initially make a loss, it can still be 'ringfenced' in a separate company without losing loss relief if the new company is owned by your existing company.

Partnerships

The other issue is that if the individuals who own A and B are themselves partners, then the two companies would be associated. So you would need to ensure that the individuals are not business partners in a personal capacity when considering the corporate partnership structure.

What else?

You should also ensure that there is a partnership agreement in place between the two companies to govern how the profits and capital gains etc., are to be split.

Chapter 5

How Much Salary in 2013/2014?

Dividends are usually the preferred way to extract cash from a company. This is now especially the case, as the higher and marginal rates of corporation tax are being reduced (thus reducing the tax benefit of paying a salary).

However, for many small company owners (profits under £300,000) it will generally make sense to pay a salary equal to the employee's national insurance earnings threshold (£7,755 for 2013/14).

This will be tax free for the director because there is no income tax or employee's national insurance. Furthermore, the salary will be a tax deductible expense for the company resulting in a corporation tax saving of £1,551 (£7,755 x 20%).

So a small salary is even better than tax free, it produces a tax deduction for the company!

Employer's national insurance kicks in on salaries over £7,696, so there will be a small amount of this tax to pay:

Employer's NI = £59 x 13.8% = £8

However, the corporation tax relief on the additional salary and on the employer's national insurance outweighs the cost:

Tax relief = £59 + £8 x 20% = £13

Larger Companies

From April 2013, when a company's profits exceed £300,000, it pays corporation tax at a marginal rate of 23.75% on the excess.

For owners of these companies, it will often be worth paying a salary equal to the personal allowance of £9,440 in 2013/14. Why? The corporation tax relief at 23.75% will outweigh the national insurance charges.

Optimal Salaries for all Company Owners?

These are not necessarily the optimal salaries for ALL company owners. For some, the optimal salary will be affected by how much income the director has from other sources and how much money is being extracted from the company.

In many cases, a salary of £7,000 is used. Not only is this a nice round number, but there is no national insurance to worry about and often no income tax.

Employer's national insurance only kicks in when your salary exceeds £7,488, employee's national insurance kicks in when your salary exceeds £7,605 and income tax usually kicks in when your income exceeds £9,440. A salary of £7,000 could escape all three taxes.

Although using a salary of £7,000 is ideal for the purposes of this guide – it is not necessarily the *optimal* salary for every company owner.

However, whether we use a salary of £7,000 or £7,755 or £9,440 will probably not make a huge amount of difference to the average business owner.

Chapter 6

Ways to Reduce Corporation Tax

Reducing corporation tax is not like reducing capital gains tax. There is not a whole host of reliefs and exemptions that you can plough through to see if any apply.

Many of the reduction opportunities relate to reducing the profits. It sounds simple but achieving this in practice is not straightforward.

The following are some of the top ways to reduce your corporation tax bill:

Make Pension Contributions

Regarding corporation tax relief for the company, all employer contributions to registered pension schemes can in principle attract tax relief without limit. I.e., they are not restricted by the employee's annual allowance, just as for any other expenses, pension contributions need to be incurred wholly and exclusively for the purposes of the trade to qualify for a tax deduction.

The Revenue view on this is that if an employee is not connected with the employer, then contributions would usually qualify for relief on the basis that the payments were for a business purpose. If the employee is connected to the employer, e.g., a director in the company, the position is less straightforward.

Directors in small companies have significant flexibility in regards extracting cash from a company, and making substantial pension contributions with only a low salary is a very tax efficient method of extraction.

For the company to qualify for a tax deduction, as stated above, the contribution needs to be wholly and exclusively for the trade.

So, unless there is a non business purpose, the pension contribution would be allowable. One of the ways that the Revenue can argue there is a non business purpose is when there is a substantial pension/salary package in relation to the services provided. HMRC have stated:

'...One situation where all or part of a contribution may not have been paid wholly & exclusively for the purposes of the trade is where the level of the remuneration package is excessive for the value of the work undertaken by that individual for the employer...'

If you can show that the contribution and salary package paid is in line with what would have been made for an unconnected employee in a similar situation, it should qualify for tax relief.

You would therefore need to raise an argument that any salary and pension contributions were incurred by the company wholly and exclusively for the purposes of the trade, and there was no non-business motive.

In essence, when looking at the tax deduction of the pension contribution in the company, the key issue is the size of the remuneration package from the company when compared to the value of the work undertaken by that individual.

As always, it is a question of fact, but the level of salary and pension would need to be reviewed as part of a total remuneration package as well as the duties/services provided.

Capital allowances

For small companies, the new capital allowance regime is very generous. When calculating the profits for accounting purposes, any capital expenditure is excluded. So any assets you buy do not reduce your profits. They do not affect the amount of corporation tax on those profits. Instead, assets are held on the balance sheet. The reasoning behind this is that the capital expenditure benefits a business for years to come (i.e. an 'enduring benefit') and is not just restricted to the current accounting period.

However, the tax provisions make available separate corporation tax relief.

The Chancellor has stated that there will be an increase in the Annual Investment Allowance to £250,000 for two years from 1 January 2013.

This applies to 'plant & machinery' expenditure. There are other allowances that apply e.g., for cars, etc.

Plant & machinery will include many assets that are purchased for the purpose of a trade excluding cars and property (unless the property expenditure is directly related to the setting for the trade).

In recent years, the rate has moved from £50,000 to £100,000 down to £25,000 and now up to £250,000. HMRC has now issued guidance notes which say this is a temporary increase and noting that the rate will drop back to £25,000 from 1 January 2015.

The allowance is allocated based on the date of expenditure, and the allowance for an accounting period which straddles the date of the rate change is pro-rated accordingly.

This means that a company with an accounting period ending 31 March 2013 will be entitled to an allowance as follows:

9/12 x £25,000 = £18,750

3/12 x £250,000 = £62,500

Total available allowance = £81,250

It is important to note that only the expenditure incurred after the rate change will be covered by the new higher allowance. The Annual Investment Allowance available for expenditure incurred in the nine months to December 2012 will be limited to £25,000.

Writing down allowances at 18%/ 8% will be available on the amount exceeding the entitlement to Annual Investment Allowance.

You should therefore carefully review the capital expenditure on the balance sheet and assess whether you will get capital allowances to reduce corporation tax.

Provisions

A provision made in accounts is the recognition of an expense or liability, the timing or amount of which is uncertain. So it will essentially get a tax deduction for expenditure before you have incurred it.

A provision made in accounts will only be allowable if:

- The business is under a present legal or constructive obligation to make the payments.
- The obligation is as a result of a past event, and
- It is probable that there will be a ' transfer of economic benefits' arising from the obligation. (I.e. the company will incur a cost).

Example of provisions that are allowable for tax purposes (as stated by the Revenue) include:

- In the period of sale for the cost of work under a warranty which a trader gives on the sale of merchandise (or under consumer protection legislation),
- for commission refundable by an insurance intermediary on the lapse of a policy where the commission is recognised as income at the inception of the policy,
- by builders for rectification work, including retentions up to the level that these have been recognised as income within accounts,
- for future maintenance of plant and machinery

Home expenses

The home is used by many companies and could be where the company actually carries out its activities (e.g., a one man consultancy company).

Even if the company carries on most of its business elsewhere, it is still entitled to a corporation tax deduction for part of the household expenses, provided that there are times when part of the home is used solely for business purposes.

Many of the bills for household expenses cover both business and private use. The part of the cost attributable to business use is allowable for tax purposes. It would then need to be recharged to the company for the company to qualify for a corporation tax deduction (e.g. by also crediting it to a directors' loan account).

You clearly need to apportion any expenses between private and business use. The types of things you may consider here are:

- Area: what proportion is used for business purposes?
- Usage: how much is consumed (e.g., where there is a metered supply such as electricity)?
- Time: how long is it used for business purposes?

There are, of course, many other tax deductions to consider. Some of the key lesser known ones include incidental costs of loan finance for companies and double tax relief. We look at these shortly.

Chapter 7

Financing a New Company Tax Efficiently

When a new company is set up, it is usually the case that cash needs to be transferred to it for the purchase of stock and materials and to cover running costs or to purchase property.

There are two main ways that this can be structured.

First, it can be as an equity injection - which usually means a purchase of share capital.

Alternatively, it can be via debt. There is much 'middle ground' with funding options that are partly debt or partly equity. Thisis the main distinction.

Why debt is often best

Very often Entrepreneurs transfer the cash to the company and leave it outstanding on loan account. (I.e. the company owes the Entrepreneur the funds). In terms of bookkeeping, the entry would be Dr. Cash, Cr Creditors.

By having the cash structured as a loan this means that the shareholder can extract the cash from the company as they wish free of income tax and national insurance. This is because you can class extractions up to the initial funding as a repayment of a loan and therefore tax free.

You could charge interest to the company on the loaned funds if you wished.

This interest would typically be tax deductible for the company, but would be taxed on you personally (but would not be subject to national insurance).

For many, this is a very attractive method of financing the new company. You can usually finance it with as much debt as you wish. There are provisions that apply an arm's length basis where one if outside the scope of UK tax (e.g., where the investor is non-resident); however, for UK residents the restrictions are minimal.

One of the main disadvantages is if the company is making losses and is to be wound up.

The tax implications of debts can be complex. Most debts are classed as simple debts, and as such, there is no gain on the disposal of the debt, but similarly there is no loss if the debt becomes irrevocable. Therefore, there would be no tax relief in this case for the loss of the loan funding in the company.

However, there are special rules that apply where a loan is made to a trader. In this case, the tax legislation allows special loss relief. In order to qualify the loan:

- must have been for money,
- must have been made, to a borrower resident in the UK; and
- must have been used wholly for the purposes of the borrower's trade, or, provided that the trade is actually carried on subsequently, for the purposes of setting it up. Loans made where the borrower never commences a trade will not qualify.
- must not be between spouses or between companies in the same group
- must not be assigned

If these conditions are satisfied, a capital loss can be treated as arising at the date of the claim.

Therefore in principle, providing any loan was made to your company for the purposes of carrying on a trade, it should be possible to ensure that the debt that is irrevocable is classed as a capital loss. Note that if the company were an investment company (e.g., a property investment company), no tax relief would be available.

This loss is a capital loss and as such can only be offset against capital gains, not income. Therefore, if you realized a gain on the disposal of an asset (e.g., shares, property etc.), the loss could be offset against any capital gains in the current year, as well as in future years.

What is the position with equity/share capital financing?

Investing cash as share capital is treated as part of the base cost of the shares for tax purposes. If the company is wound up, such would usually crystallise a capital loss equivalent to the original cost (assuming no proceeds).

However, if the shares were unquoted and if they were subscribed for directly from the company it would be possible to treat the loss as an income loss. For many, this would be most attractive as it would allow the loss to be offset against other income such as employment or dividend income.

By contrast, if the initial funding was as a loan account you would be looking at a capital loss at best.

Of course, the downside in acquiring share capital is that it would not allow an opportunity for the tax free extraction of cash from the company. You would be looking at a dividend extraction with an effective 25% tax charge for higher rate taxpayers (although basic rate taxpayers would not suffer any further income tax).

Chapter 8

Using a Directors Loan Account to Reduce Tax

A director's loan account can be very attractive in reducing UK tax. Essentially, it applies where the company owes you money. It is shown as a creditor in the accounts and you can extract funds from this as and when you choose free of income tax and national insurance.

When you owe the company, there are some nasty avoidance rules which can mean that the company has to pay a 25% tax , and you are also subject to tax on the interest free or low interest element.

These provisions though do not apply where the loan is from you to the company. You can make the loan interest free or have it as a full commercial interest bearing loan. Whatever the position, the loan repayments are still free of tax for you.

If it is an interest bearing loan, the interest element will be treated separately. The interest would be allowed as a tax deduction under the loan relationship provisions (effectively giving you a corporation tax deduction). However, it would then be subject to income tax in your hands.

When will a director's loan account arise?

It will occur whenever you transfer any asset or undertake services for the company and do not receive full consideration.

If you transferred a car to the company which was valued at £5,000, you may not take any funds from the company to represent the £5,000 value. In this case, you could either show this as a debt from the company or simply as a form of capital contribution by you.

Therefore the company would hold an asset at £5,000 and would either show a credit to loan account of £5,000 or a capital credit to the shareholders' funds of £5,000. If a debt is established, it allows the repayment to be made in the future free of tax.

It is for this reason that in many cases, a sale - rather than a gift may be preferred. What you will have to beware of though is if you gift business assets, you can often claim gift relief to defer any capital gain arising on the transfer. However, gift relief is restricted or even eliminated where some proceeds are received.

You therefore need to be very careful when deciding whether to sell for full consideration or to gift for nil consideration.

One of the key occasions when a director's loan account arises is on the incorporation of a business. This simply means that the business is transferred to a company.

In this case, the business owner could sell the business to the company for full market value. They would pay capital gains tax on the transfer at 18%/28% or 10% if Entrepreneurs Relief were available.

The proceeds could be left outstanding if the company did not have the immediate funds, and the shareholders/directors could then extract free of income tax as and when they chose.

They would therefore potentially suffer an immediate 10% CGT charge (if Entrepreneurs Relief applied) but save income tax at up to 45%.

If they did not want to suffer any CGT charge on the transfer, they could claim gift relief. However by gifting the business, no loan account would be established. Often business owners will gift part of the business and sell the remainder at full value.

Use could always be made of the annual exemption. For instance, an asset valued at £100,000 but with a £20,000 gain could be put into joint names of a husband and wife and transferred to the company. The gain would be more or less offset by the annual CGT exemptions, and the £100,000 could then be extracted free of tax.

Any transfer of assets to a company should therefore always be considered in terms of the potential impact on the loan account. If you can also arrange for a tax free transfer into the company, you have achieved a 'double whammy' in tax terms as it will be completely free of tax.

Chapter 9

Maximising Tax Relief on the Purchase of Business Premises

Buying a business property is classed as an asset for tax purposes. This means that you will not obtain tax relief for the cost of the property purchase because it is 'capital' expenditure for both tax and accounting purposes. As such, the property cost is held on your balance sheet as a 'fixed asset'.

This is completely different from the case of a property trader. A property trader buys and sells property as its main business. As such, the property is not an 'asset;', it is more like trading stock, The cost of property is not reflected on the balance sheet, but it is deducted when calculating the taxable profit of the business.

This difference is crucial as it means that businesses buying business premises will not be entitled to any tax relief for the cost of buying the property because it is capital expenditure.

Note the 'cost' of the property not only includes the actual acquisition cost of the property, but also other costs involved in the purchase (e.g. stamp duty and conveyancing fees).

You will eventually get tax relief for the costs of buying the property, but this will be at the time the property is sold. At this point, any uplift in value from the cost of purchase would be classed as a capital gain and potentially subject to tax.

You may not however sell the property for a number of years, and if the cost of buying the property is not allowable immediately, what tax relief can you get on the actual purchase?

The options for obtaining tax relief are limited. The main deductions are listed below:

Interest and finance costs

Finance costs are deductible from trading profits generally on the same basis as they are deducted in the accounts.

Deductions for finance costs

Purchasing property will give rise to a number of legal and other professional costs.

The purchase of business property will give rise to a number of costs which may not be deductible from taxable income. Generally, these costs would be of a capital nature and can not be deducted from profits for tax purposes.

In such cases, you need to identify those expenses which are associated directly with the borrowing and to exclude any expenses incurred in connection with the acquisition of the property.

It is essential to make the allocation as any legal and professional fees that are part of the funding exercise can be deducted from taxable income. This is under the deduction for 'incidental costs of obtaining finance or repaying a loan'.

The costs normally allowable include:

- Legal and professional expenses for negotiating the loan and preparing the documents.
- Underwriting commissions, brokerage and introduction fees.
- Land Registry fees, search fees and valuer's fees incurred in connection with the security for the loan.
- Commitment fees for an undertaking to make a loan available.
- Commissions for guaranteeing a loan.
- The costs of 'rolling over', extending, replacing, varying the terms of, or changing the security on, an existing loan.

You would be able to offset costs such as:

Interest payable

Premium/discount on redemption of the loan

Costs of obtaining loan finance

- Abortive expenses in connection with a loan facility that is never drawn.
- Termination costs of repaying loan finance.
- Any other payments made under the terms of a loan including payments to reimburse a lender's costs or vary the terms of a loan.

Given the wide scope of the deduction for traders on finance costs, it makes sense for any fees to be allocated as much as possible to the funding of the building. The fees will then be deductible. If the finance is substantial, it is therefore worthwhile liaising with any professionals supplying their services in relation to a property acquisition to ensure they allocate an appropriate proportion of their fees to the funding exercise.

Remember that the actual legal and other costs of the purchase will not be deductible. Only the funding element will be deductible.

Interest deduction

The deduction for interest will be one of the most significant deductions in many property purchases. The trader would get tax relief for this given it is incurred 'wholly & exclusively' for the purposes of the trade. Note that companies have a separate set of rules that apply to how interest is taxed/deducted on them. These are the 'loan relationship' provisions. In general, although the rules differ, they still get tax relief against their profits.

If you have excess finance/interest costs, this would be offset against other income and then carried forward/back.

Capital allowances

Another notable opportunity for tax relief is to claim capital allowances.

Capital allowances are available on a capital expenditure incurred by a person carrying on a 'qualifying activity' on plant & machinery that was acquired for that purpose.

A trade is a qualifying activity.

Allowances are fixed at 18% of the cost per year (after April 2012) but you will be likely to get 100% relief on expenditure up to the £250,000 annual investment allowance for 1 January 2013 – 1 January 2015.

It can therefore prove very tax efficient to carefully ascertain the costs that will qualify for plant & machinery allowances (certainly at the 100% rate, but also at the 18% plant & machinery rate).

The problem is in ascertaining exactly what is plant/machinery, and what is simply the structure. The former is allowance whilst expenditure that relates to the building structure would not be allowable.

HMRC does provide a list of various types of expenditure which they regard as not being automatically excluded from a capital allowance claim. Some of the key items of expenditure include:

- Manufacturing or processing equipment; storage equipment (including cold rooms); display equipment; and counters, checkouts and similar equipment

- Cookers, washing machines, dishwashers, refrigerators and similar equipment; washbasins, sinks, baths, showers, sanitary ware and similar equipment; and furniture and furnishings

- Sound insulation provided mainly to meet the particular requirements of the qualifying activity

- Computer, telecommunication and surveillance systems (including their wiring or other links)

- Refrigeration or cooling equipment

- Fire alarm systems; sprinkler and other equipment for extinguishing or containing fires

- Burglar alarm systems

- Strong rooms in bank or building society premises; safes

- Partition walls, where moveable and intended to be moved in the course of the qualifying activity

- Decorative assets provided for the enjoyment of the public in hotel, restaurant or similar trades

- Advertising hoardings; signs, displays and similar assets

Whether any of these would actually qualify would depend on whether they were actually required for the purposes of the trade.

You will see that careful allocation of the costs of the purchase of a building can reap dividends. Capital allowances can be lost simply because of an inappropriate description or allocation of the amounts involved.

Many large companies take great care over this and ensure that the purchase consideration is allocated in the acquisition agreement to show the amounts allocated to the relevant qualifying expenditure (fire alarm, burglar alarm etc.).

Remember the professional fees as well. Any fees that you can allocate to the capital allowance claim would also qualify for allowances. So the fees of mechanical and electrical engineers may well be linked to the installation of plant and would therefore qualify.

In some cases, 40-50% of the purchase price of modern buildings is attributable to qualifying fixtures & equipment eligible for capital allowances.

Repairs after purchase

If you buy a property in poor condition, as a general rule, you will be able to deduct the costs of repairs. The fact that you bought the property not long before the repairs are made does not in itself make the repair a capital expense.

There are though occasions when HMRC may argue otherwise (i.e. that the expenditure is capital and therefore not deductible). This would include cases where you have an agreement to renovate the property or where there is a very substantial deduction as the property is in a dilapidated state.

Provisions for repairs

You can also deduct a repairs provision where you have a liability to pay for the work, but payment has not been made at the year end. This would then reduce the taxable profits even though payment has not yet been made.

Note though you need to have incurred a liability to pay, and you will not therefore get a deduction for repairs that you think you may incur in the future.

Chapter 10

Transferring Property Assets Out Of a Company Tax Efficiently

A common scenario is for a company to hold both trading and investment assets. Maybe the shareholders have decided to use retained cash in the company to purchase investment properties or other investment assets (in the belief that this reduces the tax charge for extracting funds from the company).

Alternatively, it may simply be because of assets that were previously used for trading purposes (e.g., property) are now held as an investment.

What about the future disposal of either the property or the trade?

Taking a disposal of the trade, there would usually be no problem. The shareholders could consider a sale of the shares in the company. This can be tax efficient. Entrepreneurs Relief will often reduce the tax rate to 10%.

However, many purchasers will not want to buy a company complete with the property investment assets. Therefore, think about extracting these from the company prior to a disposal. In addition, having an investment asset in the company that is 'substantial' could prevent Entrepreneurs Relief from applying, and the CGT rate could be increased to 28%.

It is usually advised to separate the investment from the trading activities. How you actually do this without paying a fortune in tax though is another question.

A simple transfer of the property from the company to the shareholders or another company would be a disposal by the original company. As such, a gain would arise based on the market value of the property (usually). If the shareholders are UK resident, the transfer at undervalue would also be taxed on them as though they had received a dividend. This would then be subject to income tax on the element of undervalue.

All in all, this is not a good option.

Another option which may be preferable is to consider a demerging of the existing company, with the separation of the trading and the investment activities.

There are specific tax provisions that provide for CGT reliefs on a demerger applicable to trading companies, or the insolvency act could be used. The existing trading company could probably be liquidated during this process, and the assets split into new companies.

Consequently, the existing company is placed in liquidation and in essence, the liquidator transfers the assets to new companies established by the shareholders, in exchange for the issue of shares to the shareholders (e.g. X Ltd & Y Ltd).

They could then dispose of the shares in X Ltd directly without the need to crystalize a gain on Y Ltd. This treatment can also apply for investment assets. The shares in X and Y Ltd would be treated as being owned for the same holding period as that of the existing trading company.

Therefore, Newco X could receive the Investment property and Newco Y could receive the trading assets. The newcos would remain owned by the existing shareholders. They could then sell the trading company separately from the investment asset/company. Note that these are all complex areas and should be looked at in some significant detail.

If the shareholding proportions will be the same as they were for the current company (i.e. the owners would have exactly the same percentage shareholdings in X Ltd as they currently have in the trading company), it should be, although the anti avoidance provisions would need to be reviewed in detail.

The shareholders could then dispose of the shares in X Ltd or Y Ltd. A gain would arise and Entrepreneurs Relief could apply.

This would still represent a significant tax saving in many cases when compared with a company disposal of assets. (At the same time, clearly specific facts should be considered, e.g., the base cost of shares/assets, any capital losses, etc.).

If you plan to split an existing trading company, a demerger could be considered. Note that ideally this should be done during a significant period before a disposal of the shares to a third party purchaser. Even so, if necessary, the liquidation route may be considered for disposals shortly after the reorganisation.

Chapter 11

Making Your Company Investor Ready for EIS Relief

If you are looking to attract investors to your company, an added incentive for them will be if they can get tax relief on their investment. The key opportunity for relief will be under the Enterprise Investment Scheme ("EIS").

Tax Reliefs on Offer

There are five types of relief available under the EIS, relating to income tax, capital gains tax, loss relief, capital gains tax deferral relief and inheritance tax relief.

- Income tax relief is available for individuals who subscribe for new shares in an EIS qualifying company. The relief is available at 30 per cent of the cost of the shares up to £500,000. This is increased to £1M for shares issued after 5 April 2012.

- There is a carry back facility where shares subscribed in one tax year can be set against the income tax liability for the previous year. Relief cannot be carried forward.

- Capital gains tax will not be payable on any gain on the shares if they are held for a qualifying period (see below).

- If the shares are disposed of at a loss, the investor can elect that the loss (less any income tax relief already claimed) be set against any other income for that year, or the previous year, instead of being set against any capital gains.

- The payment of tax on a capital gain can be deferred where the gain is re-invested in the shares of an EIS qualifying company. The deferral is available up to one year before or three years after the gain arose. There is no minimum or maximum value or holding period, and it does not matter if the investor is connected with the company.

- Because of the interaction with Business Property Relief, shareholdings in companies that qualify for the EIS may fall outside the scope of the inheritance tax regime after two years.

Can The Investor Qualify?

- The shares issued to the investor must be paid up in full in cash on issue and must be "full risk" ordinary shares with no preferential rights to dividends, or to the company's assets on a winding up.

- If the company puts in place any arrangements to protect the investors from the risks of investing in the company or for the purchase of the shares after the qualifying period, then the investor will not be able to benefit from the tax reliefs. Investors should note that the reliefs are only available for new issues of shares and not purchases.

- The shares must be held for three years from the date of issue, or three years from the date that the qualifying trade started if this is after the shares are issued, for the income tax and capital gains tax reliefs to be available.

- An investor will not be eligible for income tax relief or capital gains' tax exemption if he is connected with the company. An investor is deemed to be connected if he is a director (unless the business angel exemption applies - see below) or an employee of the company. This restriction applies if the investor was connected during the two year period prior to the shares being issued and three years after the issue.

- An exemption applies to directors who do not receive (and are not entitled to) any remuneration for holding the post.

- The "business angel" exemption applies to investors who subsequently become paid directors if:

  - The investor is not connected to the company when the shares are issued, and the later directorship is the only connection;

  - The investor had not previously been involved in carrying on the trade the company is involved in; and

  - The investor's pay as director is reasonable.

- An investor will also be connected if he alone or together with associates holds more than 30 per cent of the share capital (or share and loan capital taken together), or more than 30 per cent of the voting rights,or is entitled to more than 30 per cent of the assets of the company on a winding up.

- The shares must be subscribed for genuine commercial reasons and not for tax avoidance purposes.

Will The Company Qualify?

The company will have to satisfy the following key criteria:

- It must not be traded on the London Stock Exchange's Main Market or any other recognised stock exchange. The AIM and PLUS markets are not considered to be recognised exchanges, and so a company listed on these markets may still qualify. The company must not be controlled by another company, and there must not be arrangements in place for this to happen.

- If the company has subsidiaries, it must own more than 50 per cent of each one (or 90 per cent in the case of a property management subsidiary).

- It must be a "small company," i.e., have gross assets of less than £15 million before the investment and £16 million afterwards for shares issued on or after 6 April 2012.

- It must be either a company carrying on a qualifying trade or the parent company of a trading group, but it must own 90 per cent of the subsidiary carrying on the qualifying trade.

- It must not raise more than £5m in any 12 month period from the three venture capital schemes (EIS, Corporate Venturing Scheme and Venture Capital Trusts).

- The trade for which the money has been raised must be carried on wholly or mainly in the United Kingdom. (This will be changed in the forthcoming Finance Act so that the company only requires a permanent UK establishment). Many trades qualify for the relief; although, a company will not be eligible where more than 20 per cent of its activities are "excluded activities" (see below).

- The investment funds can be used for the purpose of preparing to carry on a trade (including research and development), but any such trade must start within two years of the shares being issued.

- The shares must be subscribed for genuine commercial reasons and not for tax avoidance purposes.

Excluded Activities

The following activities are excluded:

- Dealing in land, in commodities or futures in shares, securities or other financial instruments;

- Dealing in goods, other than in an ordinary trade of retail or wholesale distribution;

- Financial activities such as banking, insurance, money-lending, debt factoring, hire-purchase financing or any other financial activities;

- Leasing or letting assets on hire, except in the case of certain ship-chartering activities;
- Receiving royalties or licence fees (though if these arise from the exploitation of an intangible asset which the company itself has created, that is not an excluded activity);
- Providing legal or accountancy services;
- Property development;
- Farming or market gardening;
- Holding, managing or occupying woodlands, any other forestry activities or timber production;
- Shipbuilding;
- Coal production;
- Steel production;
- Operating or managing hotels or comparable establishments or managing property used as an hotel or comparable establishment;
- Operating or managing nursing homes or residential care homes, or managing property used as a nursing home or residential care home; and
- Providing services to another person where that person's trade consists, to a substantial extent, of excluded activities, and the person controlling that trade also controls the company providing the services.

Qualifying Requirements

The company must comply with the above criteria on an ongoing basis in order for investors to benefit from the tax reliefs for the three year qualifying period.

Chapter 12

Qualifying for the New SEIS

The Government has launched a new Seed Enterprise Investment Scheme (SEIS) aimed at encouraging investment in very small, new companies. SEIS has many similarities with the Enterprise Investment Scheme (EIS), but there are significant differences.

Tax relief available under SEIS

Income tax relief

- Individuals who make qualifying investments will benefit from income tax relief equal to 45 per cent of the amount invested. However, the relief is subject to an annual subscription limit of £100,000 (i.e., a maximum tax saving of £45,000). Investors can use the relief against their tax liability for the tax year in which they subscribe, the preceding tax year, or split the relief between the two years.

Capital gains tax (CGT) reliefs

- Whenever an investment in shares benefits from income tax relief under SEIS, any disposal of those shares will also exempt from CGT, provided that the shares have been held for at least three years and the SEIS conditions have been met throughout that period.

- Chargeable gains arising on the disposal of other capital assets during the 2012/13 tax year were exempt from CGT, if, and to the extent that the investor made a qualifying SEIS investment equal to all or part of the gain and claims SEIS reinvestment relief. For 2013/2014 this relief has been carried on but only for 50% of any gain reinvested.

- Where shares are sold at a loss, the allowable loss for CGT purposes is reduced to take account of any income tax received. In some circumstances, the allowable loss will be eligible to set against income.

Eligibility and conditions

Who can benefit?

- SEIS tax reliefs apply to qualifying investors who subscribe for relevant shares in qualifying companies where all the applicable conditions are satisfied.

Who is a qualifying investor?

- The investor must be an individual who is making the investment on his own behalf (though he may invest via a nominee).

- Neither the investor, nor any of his associates, may be an employee of the investee company/group at any time during the period from the issue of the relevant shares to the third anniversary of that issue, (referred to as "Period B" in the draft legislation).

- However, where a person is a director of a company, he will not count as an employee for this purpose. Thus, an executive or non-executive director of a qualifying company can make SEIS investments. However, unless he is an unpaid director, he may be able to make follow on investments under EIS; the rules are complex and, if this could be an issue, advice should be taken.

- The investor must not have a "substantial interest" in the investee company at any time during the period from incorporation of the investee company to the third anniversary of the issue, of the relevant shares (referred to as "Period A" in the draft legislation). In summary, the investor must not alone or with his associates hold directly or indirectly, or be entitled to acquire, more than 30 per cent of the ordinary share capital; issued share capital or voting rights of the investee company; or any of its subsidiaries or be entitled to more than 30 per cent of the assets on a winding up.

What are relevant shares?

- Relevant shares are ordinary shares with no right to be redeemed, no preferential rights to assets on a winding up, and whose preferential rights to dividends (if any at all) comply with strict rules. This includes not being dependent on a decision of the company, or the investor or any other person, and not being cumulative rights where unpaid dividends are carried forward for payment in a later year.

- The shares must be:

    1. Subscribed for wholly in cash and fully paid up when issued;
    2. Issued on or after 6 April 2012 and before 6 April 2017. In other words, the Government currently intends that SEIS will have a 5-year shelf life; and
    3. Issued to raise money for a qualifying business activity to be carried on by the issuing company or a 90 per cent subsidiary. A qualifying business activity is carrying on of a new qualifying trade (see below); or preparing to carry on a new qualifying trade; or undertaking research and development from which it is intended to derive a new qualifying trade or benefit a "new qualifying trade".

- The concept a "**new qualifying trade**" is central to SEIS and includes the following features:

    1. The trade must be a qualifying trade (i.e., one which does not include, wholly or to a substantial extent, excluded activities). The definition of "excluded activities" is the same for EIS and SEIS and includes activities such as dealing in land, certain property-backed trades (such as property development and farming) and certain financial trades;
    2. The trade must be less than two years old. If the trade in question was carried on by the relevant company, or by any other person, more than two years prior before the date of issue of the relevant shares, it will not count as a new qualifying trade; and

3. The trade must be the company/group's first trade. A trade will not be a new qualifying trade if, prior to its commencement, either the issuing company or one of its subsidiaries has carried on any other trade.

What is a qualifying company?

- The company must, if a single company, exist for the purpose of carrying on a new qualifying trade. If the company is the parent of a group, the group's business must not consist to a substantial extent (i.e., 20 per cent or more) in non-qualifying activities (that is, trading activities which do not qualify for EIS or SEIS or non-trading activities).

- The company (or, if applicable, the group) must:

  1. Have gross assets which do not exceed £200,000 immediately before the relevant shares are issued;
  2. Have fewer than 25 full-time equivalent employees when the relevant shares are issued.

- The company must not have raised funds under the EIS or Venture Capital Trust ("VCT") regimes before or on the day on which the relevant shares are issued for SEIS purposes. Also note that once SEIS money has been raised, EIS or VCT money can only be raised ... once 70 per cent of the SEIS money has been spent.

- The company:

  1. must not be controlled by any other company (or any other company and any person connected with that other company);
  2. must not have any subsidiary which is not a "qualifying subsidiary" (broadly, a genuine subsidiary);
  3. must have a permanent UK establishment;
  4. must be an unquoted company;
  5. and must not, when the relevant shares are issued, be in "financial difficulty", under applicable European Commission guidelines.

For each of these conditions, the times for which they must be satisfied are slightly different.

- The qualifying business activity must be carried on by the issuing company, or a 90 per cent subsidiary and neither the company nor any of its 90 per cent subsidiaries may be a member of a partnership.

Additional applicable conditions

- Funds raised under SEIS must be spent within 3 years for a qualifying business activity.

- There is a maximum limit of £150,000, which may be raised by a company under SEIS; this is not an annual threshold but a maximum amount per company.

- SEIS reliefs must be claimed, and an investor will not be entitled to make a claim for relief, until the issuing company has provided him with a "compliance certificate". The issuing company is not permitted to apply to HM Revenue & Customs for a compliance certificate until:

    1. at least 70 per cent of the money invested has been spent; and
    2. the new qualifying trade of the issuing company, or its 90 per cent subsidiary, has been carried on for at least four months.

- There are a number of anti-avoidance provisions (including a requirement that the investment be undertaken for genuine commercial reasons and a prohibition on terms of issue such as protection against the ordinary risks of investment including, for example, anti-dilution rights).

Loss of tax reliefs

- If the investor effects a disposal of the relevant shares (which includes granting a call option or receiving a put option) before the third anniversary of the date of issue, income tax relief may be clawed back in whole or in part and any chargeable gain will be subject to CGT in the normal way. If the relevant shares were issued in 2013/14 and the investor secured exemption for another chargeable gain by way of SEIS reinvestment relief, that chargeable gain shall revive in whole or in part in 2013/14.

- Complex rules, similar to those in the EIS code in relation to "value received" by the investor, mean that where the investor receives value from the issuing company or one of its subsidiaries, unless the receipt is an "excluded payment" or an "insignificant" amount, income tax relief may be clawed back in whole or in part.

Chapter 13

Should Property Developers Use a Separate Company for Each Development?

Some of the big name property developers use separate companies for each property development. In this chapter we look at whether this is beneficial in terms of reducing your tax UK taxes.

How it works

Some of the big property development companies typically structure their developments as:

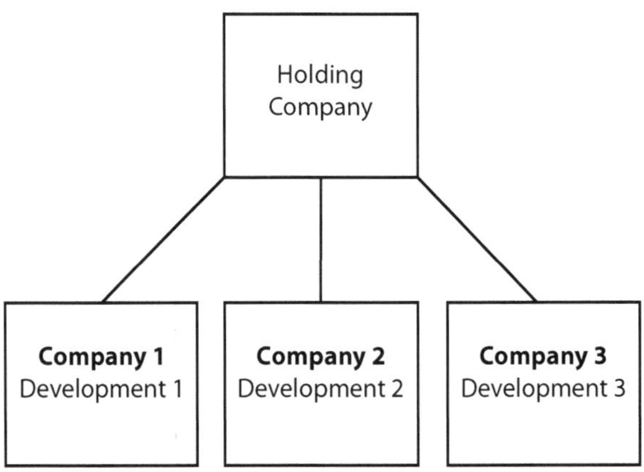

The shareholders own an interest in the holding company, and the holding company owns the shares in the underlying subsidiary companies.

There are a number of reasons for doing this:

Sale of shares

If each of the developments were undertaken in the same company (the holding company, for instance), and the shareholders wanted to sell the development to a third party seller, this would make it much more difficult. They could not just sell the shares in the company to the purchaser as the company would also contain the other development trades which the purchaser would not be buying.

If the company was to sell just development one from the company, this would crystallise either a capital gain in the holding company based on the proceeds received less the costs of the development, or it would be taxed as trading income. The latter would permit a wider range of deductions including interest on funds to finance the development. This would then be taxed in the company at rates of up to 23%. The extraction of cash as a dividend by the shareholders would then incur an income tax charge on them personally.

So what to do?

Well, this is one of the reasons why the developments are separated into different companies. If you adopted the structure as shown in the above diagram, the holding company could just sell the shares in Company 1. The key advantage of this is that the holding company could potentially qualify for an exemption for capital gains purposes on the disposal of the shares. This is by virtue of the substantial shareholdings exemption. Note that this applies providing the companies are involved in a property development trade (not investment).

The shareholders would still be subject to income on the extraction of cash as a dividend from the holding company but the avoidance of corporation tax on any capital gain would be a key incentive to using separate companies.

Joint ventures

Another advantage of establishing the different developments within different companies is that it is easier to bring in other associated partners.

Partners are often brought in on certain development, and they can be brought into the development by receiving share capital. This would then give them a share of the profits of that particular development.

If the trades were all held within one company, giving the partners shares in the main company would not be an option unless the shares were split into different classes.

Asset protection

By keeping the developments within different companies, they are keeping them legally separate. Therefore, this reduces the risk of one development being held liable for the debts of another development.

There are some advantages in keeping the companies separate. Note that as the companies would all form a group for tax purposes, they could each surrender losses and transfer capital gains within the group free of tax.

It is not always as straightforward as this. The key disadvantage of using a group of companies such as this is that it will increase the number of companies for associated companies' purposes.

Companies are associated where they are under common control. In the example above you would have four associated companies (unless the holding company was a non-trading holding company). Associated companies reduce the corporation tax bands accordingly. If there are four associated companies, this would reduce the small company band from £300,000 to £75,000 and the main corporation tax band from £1.5M to £375,000.

For many small developers the reduction in the tax bands could increase the corporation tax payable. Particularly for companies that get pushed into the marginal rate band (i.e. in the example above companies that have profits of £75,000 to £375,000). They would then be pushed into a corporation tax rate of 23.75% as opposed to 20%.

This is not an issue for the big developers because they will have profits that probably will not be impacted by the reduction in the rates in any case.

Consequently, using multiple companies for the different developments could be a good idea for the long term; however, you would need to carefully consider the impact of the additional associated companies based on your expected profits.

Chapter 14

Why It Can Make Sense for Property Investors to Use a Holding Company

Ensuring that you have the correct structure set up for your property investment or property development activities can be half the battle in terms of minimising taxes.

Many property developers hold property developments via separate companies.

Whilst this can be attractive in terms of limiting the liabilities, you need to look carefully at the tax implications.

In particular, there is a big difference between these structures:

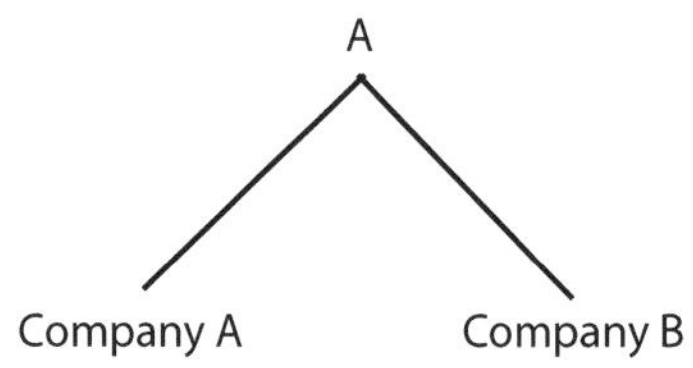

And this:

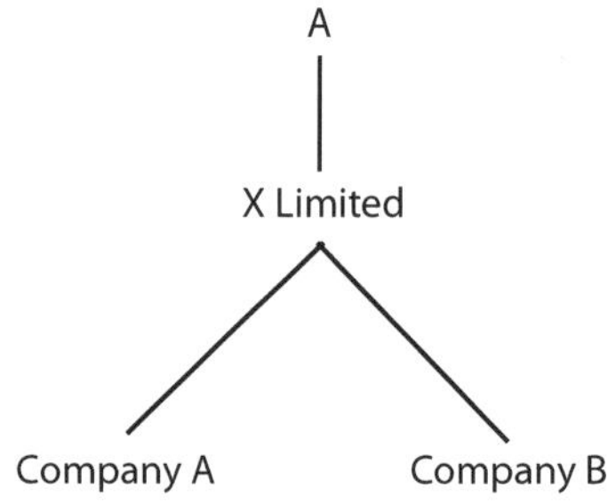

In the first instance, the individual owns the two property investment companies personally. In other words, he owns 100% of the shares in A and 100% of the shares in B.

In the second instance, the same individual owns 100% of the shares in X Limited. This individual then owned 100% of the shares in Company A and Company B.

Why use a holding company?

Many property investors structure their property investment activities as in the first example. Aside from the issue of whether a corporate structure is the best option for property investors if they do opt for a corporate structure the first structure can have some significant disadvantages - particularly if one of the companies realises a capital loss (perhaps more likely given the current economic slowdown).

In order to transfer assets between the companies' tax efficiently, they would need to form a group for capital gains' tax purposes. This effectively means that a company forms a group with its 75% subsidiaries and 75% subsidiaries of those subsidiaries, and so on. It is also required that there is at least an effective 51% ownership.

Therefore, if both A & B were owned under a holding company such as X Ltd (with the shares owned by you), this would form a group.

The key benefit of a group for capital gains tax purposes is that it can transfer an asset with a latent loss tax free to a company with a capital gain, and then crystallise the loss in the gain company. Provided the gain crystallises in the same accounting period as the loss, or in a later accounting period to which the loss is carried forward, the tax charge is only on the net gain, if any.

If there is no capital gains' group, there would be no option to offset losses between the two companies. So, you could have a situation where Company A may realise a loss, and Company B, a gain on a disposal. In this case, the loss from Company A could not be offset against the gain in Company B.

If there were a group, the loss could be used.

The group structure also allows the transfer of any rental losses between the two companies which would not apply if there were no group.

Disadvantages of using a holding company

There are though some disadvantages to using the group structure.

In particular:

- There will be an extra company for the purposes of the associated company rules. As such dependent on the level of profits in each company it could push one or more of the companies into the next corporation tax band. Of course this depends completely on the level of profits and may have no impact whatever.

- If the companies are owned directly by the shareholder, there is always the option of selling the shares in the company rather than the underlying property. This would then be taxed at 18% or 28% on the individual (or even exempt if the shareholder was non UK resident).

The holding company could sell the shares in the underlying company, but this would crystallise a capital gain in the holding company. If the subsidiary were an investment company, the substantial shareholding exemption would not be available.

This may not though be an issue if a sale of the shares wwere not on the cards.

In this case, the proceeds would be transferred free of tax to the holding company, and could be extracted by the shareholder with the same tax implications as if he held the company directly.

Chapter 15

Does It Still Make Sense to Rent Property to Your Trading Company?

Many business owners possess business premises personally and let their company trade through the premises. The main advantage to this is in terms of selling the business property separately from the business.

If the property were held by the company, you would need to arrange for a disposal by the company. This would then crystallise a capital gain on the property in the company (taxed at 20-23.75%), and there could also be a tax charge on the extraction of the proceeds by the shareholders.

Holding property personally avoids these problems, and the property owners (usually also the company shareholders) can sell the property directly.

Rent or not?

The property owners have a choice whether to charge rent to the company or not. If they do, the rent would be tax deductible for the company but would be subject to income tax for the property owners (at their marginal rate of income tax, i.e. 20% or 40%/45%).

Unfortunately along with many other adjustments from April 2008, the changes to the tax relief for disposal of businesses included a tax 'penalty' for cases where a market rental is charged.

Entrepreneurs Relief and the payment of rent

Entrepreneurs Relief replaces Taper Relief on the disposal of businesses/ shares in personal trading companies after 5 April 2008.

In the case of a property owner ('A') who holds business property in his own name which is used for the purpose of his trading company ('X Ltd'), A would only be entitled to Entrepreneurs Relief on a disposal of the business premises if it qualified as an 'associated disposal'.

There are various conditions to be satisfied; however, the property would need to be used by X Ltd for the purposes of the trade for the year before disposal.

In addition, A would need to sell the shares in X Ltd, and the disposal of the premises would need to be part and parcel of his withdrawal from the business.

Therefore A could only claim Entrepreneurs Relief against the gain on a disposal of the property if he also sold shares in X Ltd.

Assuming though that this restriction is met, there is a further restriction.

The legislation also states that where:

- only part of the assets are used for the trade
- the property is used for trading purposes for only part of the ownership period
- rent is payable from the company to the owners

... only a 'just and reasonable' amount of Entrepreneur's Relief is due.

The legislation defines this 'just and reasonable' adjustment in the context of rent by saying that you have to have regard to 'the extent to which any rent paid is less than the amount which would be payable in the open market for the use of the assets.

If a full market rental was paid, no Entrepreneurs Relief would be due; whereas, if no rent were paid in full, Entrepreneurs Relief may be due. The thinking here is that if the property were only available on the payment of rent, it is effectively an investment in the hands of A rather than being employed solely for the purposes of the business.

There can therefore be a significant disadvantage to charging a market rental to your trading company as it could prove very costly on a future disposal.

Where Entrepreneurs Relief does apply it reduces the gain on the property to 10%. If no Entrepreneurs Relief was due CGT would be charged at 28%. On a gain of £500,000 on a property disposal, renting the property to the company could therefore potentially lead to an additional CGT charge of £90,000.

What advantages are there to charging rent?

Any plan to charge rent to the company would need to carefully weigh up any tax advantages of charging the rent with the possible restriction in Entrepreneurs Relief on a future disposal.

In many cases, there may be no advantages to charging rent; however, here are some of the cases where charging rent could be beneficial in terms of reducing tax:

- Where you have a spouse who has little activity within a business, the ability to extract cash in the form of rental in their name (to utilise their personal allowance and basic rate tax band) could be advantageous. However, now that HMRC has announced a temporary suspension of the attack on income shifting, this makes the situation less important. Nevertheless, it could be important in the future

- Although rental income is subject to income tax in the hands of the property owner, it is not subject to national insurance.

This makes it preferable to extracting salary or bonus which is subject to employers and employees NIC. However, in many companies the remuneration approach is to pay small salaries to the shareholders and extract the rest by way of dividends. There is therefore no national insurance liability, and this other possible benefit of paying rent may not be applicable.

- If the company paid tax at the main corporation tax rate (23%) but the property owners were basic rate taxpayers, the 23% tax deduction in the company could be preferable to the 20% income tax charge on the shareholders

- If the property owners had taken out a substantial loan to purchase the property, the interest deduction could substantially reduce the rental profit.

The company would get a tax deduction for the rental saving tax at 20-23%, but the property may only suffer a very low tax charge on the rental profits. If no rent was charged, the interest may not obtain any tax relief.

Therefore, any decision whether or not to charge rent to your trading company needs to be carefully considered. If a disposal is on the cards in the future, the restriction in Entrepreneurs Relief could easily outweigh any benefits of charging rent.

Chapter 16

UK Corporation Tax Planning If You Leave the UK

If you trade via a UK company, the general rule is that it would be subject to UK corporation tax even if the controlling directors or shareholders were non UK resident.

As the company is a UK company it is classed as UK resident and is subject to UK corporation tax. Rates vary between 20% and 23%, however these are due to be reduced with the highest rate reducing to 21% from 2014.

Although the UK company would still be subject to UK corporation tax if the shareholders were non-resident, this doesn't mean that there aren't opportunities for UK tax planning.

Extracting cash from the company

In terms of actually extracting cash from the company this could be easily achieved by extracting dividends.

If the shareholders are non-resident they are taxed on dividends only to the extent that there is UK tax deducted at source. UK dividends have a notional tax credit of 1/9 attached, and the net effect is that non-residents can receive dividends free of UK income tax.

Therefore they can extract profits from the company free of UK tax; however, these profits will still have been subject to corporation tax in the UK company.

If the aim is to reduce the corporation tax on the company profits you would need to look at additional options.

Salary/Bonus

The simplest way is to pay salary/bonuses to employees/directors. The salary/bonus would not be subject to income tax or NIC provided the directors were non-resident and carried out the duties of employment overseas (aside from any incidental UK duties).

The company is permitted a tax deduction for all expenses incurred "wholly and exclusively" for the purposes of the trade.

Therefore in order for the company to substantiate a tax deduction for salary or bonus payments it would need to be linked to a benefit received by the company and for the purposes of its trade. This usually means that the salary/bonus payments need to be related to:

- Genuine services provided by the employees/directors to the company, and

- Calculated at an arm's length rate for those services.

Essentially you would want to be able to argue that the company would make payments even if the employees/directors were otherwise unconnected with the company (i.e. not shareholders).

You could for instance look at paying both a market value salary for the duties undertaken by non-resident directors as well as a bonus arrangement related to their specific fields of responsibility.

Offshore company

The other option would be to use an offshore structure, particularly an offshore company and recharge amounts to the UK company.

In terms of the company itself you would need to ensure:

1. It was controlled and managed from overseas. There should be no issue with this if the controlling directors and shareholders are non-resident.

2. It had no UK trade (as even if non-resident, profits from a UK trade could still be within the scope of UK tax). The location of the trade is usually where the key revenue generating activities are undertaken.

The simplest way to use an offshore company is for the directors to provide services via this to the UK company.

This is a form of a service company. Similar considerations apply as above (i.e., in terms of transfer pricing), plus you would need to ensure that the rates charged were at market levels for the services provided.

The offshore company would receive the receipts free of UK and local tax. The UK company would obtain a tax deduction for the payments.

If you were looking to transfer part of the trade to an offshore company, this could avoid UK tax. The offshore company would recharge for the services to the UK company which would be free of tax in the offshore company. A BVI or IOM company is often used for this purpose.

HMRC usually accept that a service company used to employ staff, own or lease business premises or provide other administrative services is genuine assuming that the company recharges the UK Co. at an appropriate mark up (e.g., 10-15%).

Another option would be to use an offshore holding company. You would achieve this by using a share for share exchange to place the new offshore company as the holding company of the UK company. A management recharge from the UK to the offshore company would be deductible for corporation tax purposes, but again, you would need to ensure that it relates to genuine services provided by the offshore company to the UK company. A management recharge of 100% of the profits, for instance, would not be acceptable.

Goodwill

An important issue on a transfer of any aspect of the trade would be whether there was a transfer of goodwill from the UK company.

The transfer of the trade from the UK company to the offshore company would be a disposal for capital gains purposes. This is not a specific rule that applies to transfers to offshore companies but rather is a general rule that applies to the transfer of any assets out of a company.

Therefore, irrespective of the disposal consideration that is actually transferred from the offshore company to the UK, any capital gain in the UK company would be based on the market value of the assets transferred. You would need to value the assets that were transferred to the offshore company. This would include plant/machinery, any land or property, but usually goodwill is the largest asset transferred.

However, if the value of the goodwill is represented by the personal services carried out, the directors may be able to argue that it is effectively personal goodwill. If this were the case, they may be able to argue that there was no disposal for CGT purposes.

Aside from this, a transfer of back office operations with a recharge to the UK company would usually be acceptable.

Regarding the actual transfer of the revenue generating activities, the best option could be to undertake new activities in the offshore company where there could be no argument of a transfer of goodwill. The profits would then arise free of UK tax in the offshore company.

Distribution

The other key tax issue on the transfer of the trade overseas is that the transfer would also be treated as a distribution (i.e., a dividend) to the shareholders given that they have extracted value from the company.

The amount of the distribution would be the "undervalue" at which the trade was transferred.

Note that non UK residents are only charged to UK income tax on dividends to the extent that tax was deducted at source. Given that there would be no tax deducted at source, it may be possible to avoid income tax on the distribution.

The alternative would be for the offshore company to pay the full market value to the UK company for the trade.

There would then be no distribution on the transfer, but the shareholders could extract the cash as non-residents free of further income tax.

Anti Avoidance Rules

Beginning April 2013, the new Statutory Residence Test also introduces a "temporary non residence" rule that will apply to dividends.

The new rules state that if you become non-resident and extract dividends from a UK company which represent profits that were accumulated whilst you were UK resident, you would need to be non-resident for at least five complete tax years to avoid income tax being charged on the dividends when you return.

Chapter 17

Transferring Your UK Company Overseas To Avoid UK Tax

Some of the UK's largest companies have transferred their operations overseas. In this chapter we look at how a UK company can 'migrate' overseas tax efficiently and the tax benefits in doing so.

There are many ways to structure the move overseas; however, the most drastic and also the most effective in terms of minimising ongoing taxes is to relocate the holding/principal company overseas. This is known as a company migration.

The benefit of this is that the company would be exempt from UK tax on overseas profits as well as UK and overseas capital gains.

UK trading profits would still be subject to UK tax; however, for companies with overseas operations, the tax benefits of moving abroad can be substantial. Allied to this is the fact that they can frequently transfer operations abroad to avoid having a UK taxable presence in any case.

You can then establish the company in a low tax jurisdiction such as Ireland or Cyprus with corporation tax rates as low as 12.5%/10%.

Where you have a UK incorporated company there are two main ways that it can effectively migrate:

- Firstly it can become non UK resident by virtue of having treaty residence overseas.

- Secondly, you can look to some fancy restructuring to interpose a new offshore holding company

Treaty residence

This is the only real way to completely migrate.

If the UK company is resident in an overseas country by virtue of the overseas country rules, you would need to look at the double tax treaty to see which country the company is 'treaty resident' in.

For companies, the standard double tax treaty decides the question of treaty residence by looking at which country the effective control is exercised from. If it is the UK, the company would be UK treaty resident. If it is controlled from overseas, it could be classed as treaty resident overseas. Any company that is treaty resident overseas is classed as non UK resident for UK tax purposes.

This means that the transfer of control overseas under the scope of a double tax treaty could cause a UK exit charge on the migration (as the company would be deemed to be non UK resident).

Anyone owning a UK company and planning to move overseas would need to be careful to ensure that the overseas tax position and that the position under the Double Tax Treaty was reviewed.

Exemptions from the exit charge?

Certain assets are excluded from the charge. There are two main exemptions from the exit charge:

- If the company that is migrating continues to trade in the UK through a branch or agency then, even though it has become non-resident, it will be within the charge to Corporation Tax as regards certain assets.

- Assets which are situated in the UK and are used for the purposes of the trade or branch or agency are then exempted from the exit charge. Therefore, a company that trades from the UK, and holds UK trading property (e.g., offices, warehouses, factories etc.)

would not include any uplift in value on these assets when calculating the exit charge.

- Secondly, it is possible to defer the charge on foreign assets of a foreign trade where a subsidiary company migrates, but the principal company remains resident in the UK. The charge on deemed disposals may be partly or wholly postponed if the following conditions apply immediately after the relevant time:

- assets are situated outside the UK and are used in or for the purposes of a trade carried on outside the UK ('foreign assets'), the chargeable company is a 75 per cent subsidiary of a company which is resident in the UK, the 'principal company',

- the chargeable company and the principal company elect for postponement within two years of the relevant time.

This will therefore apply where a UK subsidiary of another UK company transfers residence overseas. Any UK assets used for a UK trade would qualify for the exemption under the above provision. Any foreign assets used for an overseas trade would qualify under this provision.

Against EU law

The EU has looked at exit charges in a number of cases (e.g., the Lasteyrie case for individuals) and more recently the Cartesio case.

In early 2012, the EU issued the UK with a "reasoned opinion" requesting the UK to amend the exit charge provisions.

Now, the UK is introducing measures for the qualification process of companies that migrate from the UK to another EU or EEA member state electing, temporarily, to defer for up to 10 years ... the payment of exit charges on gains and profits ... deemed to arise when a company ceases to be UK resident.

The new measures will be effective retrospectively, allowing for elections to defer in respect of accounting periods ended on or after 10 March 2012.

As the measures were prompted by a requirement of EU law, only companies formed in accordance with the laws of an EU or EEA member state and who transfer their tax residence from the UK to another EU or EEA state qualify.

Qualifying companies may enter into an exit charge payment plan with HMRC, agreeing to a schedule of payments of tax and interest in accordance with either of two methods:

- The standard instalment method: the exit charge is payable in six equal annual instalments.

The first instalment is due nine months and one day after the end of the last accounting period in which the qualifying company is resident in the UK for tax purposes.

Repayments may, however, be accelerated in a number of scenarios, including insolvency and relocation to a state outside the EU or EEA; and

- The realisation method: the exit charge is payable in annual instalments on the basis of how the value of the various assets of the company, subject to the charge, is expected to be realised.

Qualifying companies will be required to provide HMRC with annual reports detailing the realisation of its exit charge assets and liabilities.

In all cases, the maximum number of annual instalments is ten, the first of which is due nine months and one day after the end of the last accounting period in which the qualifying company is resident in the UK for tax purposes.

There may be fewer annual instalments if the assets and liabilities in question are realised sooner.

Restructuring

The big problem with a transfer of the effective management is the exit charge on the gains in the company when it leaves the UK.

Given such difficulties, the larger corporate groups look to achieve the benefits of migration by creating an offshore holding company.

They would achieve this by interposing a new non-UK holding company between the UK company and its shareholders. I.e., the shareholders now own shares in a non-resident company, which then owns the UK company.

This is relatively straightforward and can be achieved by a share for share exchange provided the share exchange is accepted as being for bona fide commercial purposes. If not then you'd be looking at further reorganising to implement the holding company.

You would need to ensure that the holding company was genuinely managed from abroad to ensure it was not UK resident and was exempt from UK corporation tax on overseas income.

The key advantage in having an offshore holding company is that:

1. it can receive overseas income streams generally free of UK tax, and

2. it can hold shares in CFC's without being subject to the onerous CFC provisions.

The exit charge is avoided as the UK company would still be controlled from the UK, but the shareholders can obtain the benefits of the tax treatment offshore company.

It used to be advisable to implement 'income access' arrangements to allow shareholders to extract dividends from the UK company. However, now that the tax credit has been extended to UK residents on overseas dividends, for most UK shareholders this would not be necessary, and they could extract cash directly from the offshore company.

Chapter 18

Using a UK Company in Offshore Tax Planning

For many non-residents, UK entities and other tax planning vehicles have become of increasing importance when looking at structuring overseas investments.

This is in part due to the fact that the UK does not appear on any blacklists and therefore, will as a rule attract less attention from overseas tax authorities than other blacklisted countries.

The UK can be used as a stepping stone in a number of ways:

Treaty non-resident

Although a UK incorporated company is typically subject to UK corporation tax at effective rates of up to 23.75%, it can gain significant advantages if it's treaty resident overseas.

Under the provisions a company incorporated in the UK, but qualifying as a resident of some other country for the purposes of a tax treaty, is to be treated for UK tax purposes identified as not UK resident. This is clearly very attractive in terms of UK tax because a non-resident company would be exempt from UK tax on gains as well as overseas income.

In terms of overseas tax, you would need to ensure that the treaty was with a country that taxed the company profits at low or nil rates e.g.,:

- A company incorporated in the UK but resident in Mauritius may have a tax rate as low as 1.5%.

- A company resident in Singapore will pay no tax on any of its foreign income,
- A company resident in Malaysia will be exempt from tax on most foreign income
- A company resident in Barbados will pay local tax on its foreign income only if it remits income to Barbados. None of these countries levy any tax on capital gains.

Therefore, a UK incorporated company treaty resident in a suitable jurisdiction can have the best of both worlds.

UK holding company

A UK company can be very attractive as a holding company. For example, there could be an operating company, resident in a high-tax country, which is owned by an investor in a zero-tax jurisdiction. By interposing a UK holding company, dividends may be free of withholding tax or suffer a lower rate of withholding tax than would be suffered if the dividends were paid direct to the investor. This is because the UK holding company can benefit from a tax treaty or from EU the Parent/Subsidiary Directive.

The UK though has another benefit as it does not levy any tax on outgoing dividends. Consequently, the shareholders resident abroad do not need to worry about rerouting dividends or other tax planning strategies to reduce withholding taxes.

Corporate Partner

Another way of using a UK company is as the managing partner in a limited liability partnership. Partnerships are transparent for tax purposes.

Therefore, where a partner is non-resident and the partnership income has a non-UK source, the partner has no UK tax liability.

Typically, the UK company will be a form of nominee and will be entitled to only a small share of the profits under the profit sharing agreements. Most of the income will go to the overseas partners.

Customers, will however, deal with the UK partner, and may by so doing be able to circumvent blacklist and other problems.

Note that unlike a company, the tax liability is not usually affected by the "management and control" of the business.

As a result, if the partners want to have partnership meetings in London and take decisions there about the management and control of the partnership business, they can do so. They would though need to ensure that there was no UK trade. (Otherwise the profits would be subject to UK tax).

Chapter 19

Using an Offshore Subsidiary to Avoid UK Corporation Tax

Companies looking to expand overseas could use an offshore company to potentially avoid UK corporation tax.

The company would still need to be non-resident in order to avoid UK corporation tax on the foreign trade.

Therefore, it would need to have foreign directors actually operating the company at a senior level. The UK parent company would therefore need to ensure that the foreign directors actually exercised real control over the company and that they didn't just rubber stamp decisions of the UK parent company.

However, if the foreign subsidiary were non-resident, the profits from the overseas trade could potentially accumulate free of UK corporation tax in the offshore company providing the CFC rules are avoided.

Note that an offshore subsidiary is only an effective shelter if a taxable presence in high tax jurisdictions is avoided. The rules as to the extent of a taxable presence vary from country to country; therefore, local advice should be taken in the countries trades will be carried out.

What are the "CFC" Rules?

I mentioned above that a nonresident subsidiary can be attractive providing the CFC rules are avoided.

The CFC rules are therefore very important for any company that wants to set up an overseas subsidiary.

If the CFC rules apply, the UK company will have to pay tax on the overseas company's profits, provided the percentage of profits apportioned is at least 25%.

You should note that the UK CFC regime will not apply if you are an individual owning an overseas company.

Before falling within the CFC rules, a company would firstly need to meet the definition of a 'controlled foreign company'.

A controlled foreign company (CFC) is one which is resident outside the UK, controlled by persons resident in the UK.

'Control' is determined by considering the rights of the UK residents with an interest in the company, together with any rights held by persons connected with the UK resident.

Broadly, a person will have control if they have power to secure that the affairs of the company are conducted in accordance with their wishes, where that power arises through shareholdings, voting power, or by the documents governing the non-UK company.

So although the foreign subsidiary may have an overseas board of directors exercising control (to make it non-resident for UK tax purposes), given it's a subsidiary of a UK company it would fall within the CFC rules.

Purpose of the CFC Rules

The CFC regime attempts to prevent UK companies from artificially diverting profits away from the UK and into low tax jurisdictions.

Such diversion is more likely to occur in businesses where income is mobile, such as royalties, interest, consultancy fees, or where the overseas entity has large trade related connections with UK customers or suppliers.

Effectively, the taxpayer is presumed 'guilty' unless it could get itself into one of the prescribed exemptions.

If the overseas subsidiary is deemed to be a CFC, its profits are added to those of the UK company and subject to UK corporation tax.

New CFC Rules

The CFC regime has been thoroughly revamped, and the big change that will affect most readers is a £500,000 de-minimis profit limit.

This means that most small companies will fall outside the CFC regime, providing there are no arrangements designed to take advantage of this exemption.

The exemption states that the profits of a CFC with accounting profits (or assumed UK-equivalent taxable profits) of less than £500,000 and non-trading profits of less than £50,000 will be exempt from the CFC charge.

Where this exemption applies, the profits arising in the overseas company will usually be completely free of UK corporation tax – providing the profits are not extracted as dividends by the UK company.

Other Cases

Although the £500,000 exemption will apply to many companies, there will continue to be a number of small companies which are caught by the CFC rules.

For instance, take a property development company overseas which will report much of its profit in one or two years – any worthwhile investment is likely to return more than £500,000 of profit. Whilst the property project might last three to five years or so, those profits will probably get reported in one go. As a result, that entity will be a CFC (if the low tax test is met). Unfortunately the overseas entity will be within the main CFC rules.

So what can we do to avoid an apportionment of profit back to the UK parent? Let us walk through the exemptions that are proposed:

- The first test to check is probably the excluded territories exemption. The government has published a list of those jurisdictions where they are happy that the local corporation tax will be no less than 75% of the UK equivalent liability. Any companies resident in these jurisdictions will not be CFCs. We have listed those countries in Appendix I

- The next exemption will be the low profit margin test. Essentially the CFC must have a very low profit margin of less than 10% of cost. Cost cannot include any related party expenditure.

- Next, we move onto the business trading income safe harbour. Here the CFC needs to meet a variety of tests.

- These include having a business premises available locally, incurring no more than 20% of overall expenditure on supplies from UK sources, invoicing no more than 20% of total turnover to UK customers. In addition, there should be a limited connection to UK orientated intellectual property rights. The management cost of the CFC should be at least 80% incurred outside the UK.

- This safe harbour approach is helpful, but currently the rules are conceptual. There is little in the way of guidance or examples. The area of IP is one of the great uncertainties of the CFC legislation as the way in which 'connection' is determined is still largely up for debate.

- There is an exemption for CFCs that only let property in the foreign jurisdiction. There are also exemptions for incidental non trading finance income.

- There is a new exemption for finance companies set up in low tax jurisdictions which meet a number of criteria. This reduces the rate of UK corporation tax that might be levied down to just 5.25%. We will look at this in more detail later

- Overarching the CFC rules will be a 'gateway test'. This test will allow taxpayers and advisers to very quickly rule a company out of the CFC regime where it meets a number of criteria. Currently, these are largely conceptual with very little practical commentary of example of application.

Summary

The net effect of the above is if the offshore company can clearly establish management and control overseas and can avoid being caught by the CFC rules (e.g., by having overseas profits of less than £500,000), the profits generated using an overseas subsidiary can be free of UK tax.

There may of course be foreign tax charged.

In addition, if the profits are extracted out of the foreign company and paid to the UK company, there may be a tax charge on the dividend

Chapter 20

Structuring Your Business or Company Prior to a Disposal

When looking to reduce tax on the sale of your business or company, the first aspect to consider is the form of business entity and exactly what is to be sold. The form of business entity would usually be considered at the date of start up, and the essential distinction is between a UK company and the offshore company, trading personally or via a partnership.

Using a company has advantages. Not only does it provide for a measure of protection for the traders personal assets (house, investments etc.,), but it can also reduce the ongoing tax liabilities on the business profits, where some of the business profits are reinvested in the business.

As many businesses will not look to extract significant sums for a number of years, using a company could reduce the tax rate to 20%, from 40% or 45%. In addition, there could be a saving in national insurance, as the company would not be subject to NIC on profits arising, but a sole trader or partner would.

However on disposal, unless you can structure a disposal as a disposal of the shares, there could be a nasty CGT shock.

When using a company, you have two options for the disposal. You could sell the shares, or alternatively, the company could sell the assets. If you traded personally, you would simply sell the assets/trade directly. For most UK residents, a disposal personally will be much more attractive than a company disposal due to Entrepreneurs Relief. A disposal of business assets (which included shares in your personal trading companies as well as an interest in a business) reduce the CGT rate to 10% after one year. This is a massive tax benefit, and usually a company disposal could not compete.

If the company did sell the assets, not only would it not be entitled to claim Entrepreneurs relief, but it would then also need to consider extracting the cash from the company. Fine, if you are an expat because you can just take a dividend free of UK income tax, but if you are a UK resident, you will be subject to a further 25% (or 30.55% if above £150,000) income tax charge for all amounts in excess of the basic rate tax band.

Therefore if you do own a company, the best option is usually to sell the shares in the company. The gain will then arise on you, and you can try to claim Entrepreneurs Relief.

This depends on whether or not the purchaser wants to buy the shares. A problem particularly with property type businesses is that a purchaser may well see the company's assets as a short term resale opportunity.

Therefore, if they acquire the shares, they will 'inherit' the previous tax liability. Any gain since the company originally acquired the property(s) will come into charge when the property(s) is sold. In this case, although the purchaser may well agree to a share purchase, you will usually find that a discount is made for the company's tax liability up to the date of the share disposal. This will eliminate any tax benefits to you of the share disposal route.

This is important to consider when creating the original start up. If the business were personally owned, the tax savings could be substantial due to the enhanced reliefs.

Therefore, choosing the type of entity would not usually be undertaken immediately prior to a disposal unless you do business as a sole trader and want to arrange for a disposal of shares in a company, rather than a direct disposal of assets.

The main reason for this would be if you run a UK business but are also looking to emigrate from the UK personally. In this case there are some big advantages to transferring the business to a company before you leave the UK.

The reason for this is that although as a non UK resident you are exempt from UK CGT on gains, this does not apply to gains arising from a UK branch or agency trade (i.e. where there is a permanent establishment).

Therefore if you are carrying out a trade from the UK, and even if you leave the UK, you could find yourself subject to UK CGT.

A simple way around this is to incorporate the business before you leave the UK. There are some tax reliefs that allow a trading business to transfer all of its assets to a company without a tax charge. You could then leave the UK and sell the shares in the company free of UK CGT as a non UK resident.

I mentioned above that an overseas company could be used as one of the types of entities. In most cases, UK resident and domiciled individuals would achieve no tax benefit by using an offshore company. If you were planning to leave the UK or if you had overseas partners/directors, the position would be completely different. Such is true unless these apply, for MOST UK residents ... they would find obtaining tax benefits from an offshore structure difficult.

Other assets

If a company wants to sell its shares—which as we have seen above will minimise tax for many UK residents—it can not pick and choose which parts of the business are to be sold. If you own the business personally, or the company is selling the assets, you could select which assets are to be sold and which ones retained. When you sell the shares, these relate to shares in the whole company, and therefore, the whole of the business/assets, such would ensure that the company contains the parts of the business and other assets that you want to sell is very important.

This is often a problem with a company that has been used to undertake two trades or where an investment property is held in a trading company. You would then need to extract the trade that you wished to retain/property. A simple transfer of a trade or the property out of the company should be avoided as this would not only be a taxable chargeable gain. Even so, unless full consideration was payable to the company for the transfer, an income tax charge could arise on the shareholders.

There are basically two ways to achieve the transfer of assets out of the company tax efficiently.

Hive Up

This would work by the shareholder using the share for share exchange provisions to form a new holding company, and the property could be transferred out of the company free of tax.

Example

Giles owned all of the shares in Giles UK Ltd which owned a commercial property and a trading business. He could form a new company (Giles Investments) which would acquire the shares in Giles UK Ltd from Giles in return for an issue of shares by Giles Investments to Giles.

The position would then be that Giles would own the shares in Giles Investments.

The property could then be transferred free of any immediate tax charge to Giles Investments.

This would be good as Giles UK Ltd would then hold just the trading business and would be a much more attractive option for a trade purchaser.

Demerger

We have looked at this in an earlier chapter. Essentially, this can be used to split a company either where there are two trades being carried on, or where there is a trade and an investment business.

Broadly, there are two methods of carrying out a demerger.

The first utilises a specific legislation introduced for this purpose, and the second uses the insolvency legislation. Under either case, you could use these provisions to transfer assets or trades out of the company to ensure that you are selling only the assets you want to sell and the assets that the purchaser wants to buy.

Excess cash and pre sale dividend

If the company has a large cash balance, and if Entrepreneurs Relief is not due, a tax efficient option is to extract cash from the company as a dividend.

The effective tax rate on this is likely to be 25% if within the higher rate band, but at the CGT rate if the shares had been owned and would be in the region of 28%. In this case, it would then make sense to extract the cash before the disposal by way of a dividend.

Clearly if you qualified for Entrepreneurs Relief on the shares, this would be less attractive. Entrepreneurs Relief is only given to trading companies.

The Revenue will refuse to treat a company with substantial non trading assets as a trading company. Therefore, if there was a large cash balance in the company, this could in itself prevent business asset status. It would then be important to consider whether the extraction of cash as a dividend could revive business asset status a couple of years before a disposal to maximise relief.

Previous liabilities

One of the big problems with a share disposal is from the purchasers perspective, it is the 'riskiest'. They will not just be acquiring a bundle of assets and liabilities like they would under an asset deal. As the company has a separate legal entity, they will also be taking on any company liabilities.

Therefore, from the purchaser's perspective, the risk is that they will be sued for something that happened before they even owned the shares. In order to protect the purchaser, the disposal contract will be every comprehensive and include a raft of warranties and indemnities for you to sign to try and protect the purchaser as much as possible.

If this does not sound appealing you could look to a hive down to meet your and the purchaser's requirements.

A hive down is essentially a cross between an asset purchase and a share deal.

The seller company would transfer its trade and assets to a new company, and this new company is then acquired by the purchaser. It is of benefit to purchasers as it allows a share purchase but also allows them to acquire a company holding those assets and the part of the business which the seller wants to dispose of, and which the purchaser wishes to acquire. This means that it allows the purchaser to acquire a 'clean' company which does not come with any bad history and with no risk of any skeletons jumping out of the closet.

There are some special tax reliefs which can be available using the hive down route to ensure that the transfer can be made free of tax; however, the main tax advantage to the purchaser would be the ability to transfer any losses to the new company.

The goal should be to put together a package that fits in with both you and your purchasers' requirements. This could therefore include removing any surplus assets, using a newco to arrange a share disposal or arranging a hive down to provide a clean company.

This could even include a straightforward asset disposal by the company for example if:

- You were non UK resident and could extract cash from the company free of tax (subject to the new "temporary non-resident" provisions from April 2013)

- The company had large capital losses to offset any gains

- The company would be reinvesting proceeds in other business assets and could make a rollover relief claim. (This would not be available if you personally made the reinvestment, but the gain arose to the company).

Chapter 21

Qualifying for Entrepreneurs Relief When Your Company Has Large Cash Balances

On a sale of shares, you will only qualify for Entrepreneurs Relief if the company is an unquoted trading company (or the holding company of a trading group).

It is very important to determine whether a company is a trading company because this can make the difference between receiving or being denied Entrepreneurs Relief.

How Does the Taxman Define a Trading Company?

As you would expect, there is no simple answer to this question, as each case is approached differently. The tax legislation does not include much of a definition of a trading company, so it is simply down to Revenue and Customs and the courts to establish some guidelines. Thankfully, because of the significant impact that this distinction can have, Revenue has given us some general rules that can be used as a guide.

The legislation on the new Entrepreneurs Relief states that it will follow the old taper relief definition of a trading company. This states that a company is classed as a trading company provided its activities "... do not include to a substantial extent activities other than trading activities".

Provided a company does not have "substantial" non-trading activities, there should be no problem qualifying for the relief.

However, the taxman's view of 'substantial' is probably not the same as yours, and they would take this to mean more than 20% of the income or assets.

The guidance they have published on this states that they will look at a number of factors including:

- Any income from non-trading activities
- Any non-trading assets held on the balance sheet
- Time spent by directors or employees in non-trading activities

Looking at whether or not your company is a trading company, it is probably advisable to review the statutory accounts for the previous six years or so, looking at these measures for any indications of non-trading activities.

The kind of things Revenue and Customs could regard as non-trading include:

- Holding investment property via a company
- Holding shares in other companies (if your company isn't a holding company)
- Having surplus cash on the balance sheet not required for business purposes.

The surplus cash issue is a particularly nasty one, and although it's aimed at so-called 'money box' companies where cash is rolled up in a company, it can apply to genuine trading companies that happen to build up large cash reserves.

How to Get Classed as a Trading Company

The definition of trading company for Entrepreneurs Relief purposes is found in TCGA 1992 s165A(3) which states that "a company carrying on trading activities whose activities do not include to a substantial extent activities other than trading activities". HMRC interpret substantial as more than 20% and looks at the activities of the company as a whole.

The definition does refer to activities, not assets. In many cases, the company is a trading company with large cash balances which has trading turnover well in excess of 80% of the total turnover and well over 80% of employee and management time is devoted to trading activities. It is only the non trading assets that exceed 20%.

Therefore, the argument would be that there is a genuine trading activity even taking account of the surplus cash. If the cash were actively managed by you, it could be argued that this was a non-trading activity; however, this is frequently not the case. The only activity is the trading activity.

As I understand it, HMRC takes a rounded view of the different activities and transactions undertaken by the company. Providing there is a genuine trading activity, there should be a good case that the company should qualify for Entrepreneurs Relief.

However, if you wanted to be certain of the position, you would either need to consider other options such as extract the cash (at least 12 months before the disposal) or argue that the cash was required for the future purpose of the business.

When looking at the accounts for the period in question, if you do find there are substantial non-trading activities, you will then need to consider whether these can be satisfactorily explained to the tax inspector so that they don't 'taint' the status of the company. The two main exemptions from the non-trading rules are:

- Time period.

When looking at the status of the company, you would usually examine the position over the course of a number of financial years. It may well be the case that in some years the 20% threshold was exceeded, and in others it was not. In this case, it could be in your interests to take an average position over the entire period.

In such cases, HMRC have been known to accept that, although in one or two isolated years, non-trading income had been substantial, when compared with total receipts over the entire period in question the 20% threshold was not breached.

- Reasonably required for business purposes.

The other main option is to argue that although the 20% threshold has been breached, this does not amount to a non-trading activity. This would mainly apply to cash held on the balance sheet, particularly where the cash is invested.

For the cash to amount to a non-trading activity, it would need to be shown that it was not reasonably required for business purposes. Therefore, retaining the cash to avoid incurring a personal tax charge on extraction would not be a good enough reason to avoid being classed as a non-trading purpose.

If you did manage to establish that the cash was used for a business purpose, then it is unlikely that HMRC would restrict trading status. To do this, you will need to look at the specific business environment and requirements of your particular trade. It may be, for example, that you were required to retain a fixed level of cash on deposit (as in the case of bookmakers, insurance agencies and travel agencies), which would clearly be a persuasive argument that you held the cash for a business purpose. Any legal duty or recommendation from a trade association, for example, for a certain level of liquid assets would be likely to satisfy the taxman.

Similarly, if your company had sold a part of its operations and was holding the proceeds on deposit while seeking out potential acquisitions, this would also be likely to be accepted as a trading purpose. Any future business purpose could be acceptable.

Chapter 22

Tax Planning for a Disincorporation

Much has been written about the tax benefits of using a company, but what if you change your mind and want to go back to being a sole trader or partnership?

For tax purposes, this is known as 'Disincorporation', and it is well worth considering how this would be taxed—particularly as the tax position on transferring assets out of a company is much less favorable than when you are transferring assets into a company.

Transferring your business

If after incorporating your business, you decided some years down the line that you wanted to trade personally again, you would need to transfer the business back into a company.

Note that this would be a transfer of the actual assets of the business into a new company. So you would essentially need to look at the various elements of your business and consider what the tax impact would be on a transfer to a limited company.

You'd usually be looking at transferring:

- Goodwill
- Land/Property
- Stock
- Creditors/Debtors/Cash

The main problem in tax terms with 'Disincorporation' as opposed in 'Incorporation' is that there are very few tax reliefs or concessions available. The two key problems will be:

Capital Gains Tax charge

The transfer of assets from the company to shareholders would be a disposal for capital gains tax purposes. As the shareholders and company would be connected, the disposal proceeds would be deemed to be the market value, irrespective of the amount that any assets are actually transferred for.

So the company would need to obtain a valuation of any assets transferred, and it would crystallise a capital gain based on the uplift in value from the original acquisition. Frequently, this will be a big problem in terms of goodwill in the company. It is also important to note that goodwill can exist even if no value is reflected on the balance sheet.

Even if a value is shown on the balance sheet, the actual market value may be much higher. The company would then be taxed on any capital gain on the goodwill transferred at its marginal rate of corporation tax (e.g., 20% if it is within the small company tax band).

The previous method of incorporation could also be relevant here. For instance, when the original business was transferred to the company and a gift relief claim was made, any gain on the goodwill on incorporation may have been deferred.

This would then reduce the base cost of the asset held in the company. So a subsequent transfer of the asset back to the company would crystallise the original 'deferred gain' as well as any subsequent uplift in value. Unlike when you transfer a business to a company, you cannot claim gift relief when transferring assets out of a company.

Example

Let us assume Jack runs his business as a sole trader. The only asset is goodwill valued at £200,000. He decides to incorporate, and he transfers the goodwill to a company. He also claims gift relief to hold over any capital gain.

His CGT calculation on incorporation is as follows:

Goodwill	£
Market Value	200,000
Cost	-
Indexation	-
Gift Relief	-200,000
Gain	NIL

Five years later, he decides he wants to transfer his business back into his own name. The goodwill is now valued at £500,000.

The transfer of the goodwill from the company to Jack is a disposal for capital gains purposes by the company. However, the base cost of the company is NIL. This is the £200,000 value of the goodwill at incorporation, less the gift relief claimed.

This means that the full value of £500,000 would be charged as a capital gain in the company.

If Jack had chosen the 'incorporation relief' method of originally incorporating his business, the £200,000 gain would have been held over against the cost of the shares not the cost of the goodwill in the company. Such a transfer of the goodwill back into his name would have only crystallised a capital gain of £300,000. This is because the base cost of the goodwill would be £200,000 and not NIL.

The CGT charge on transfer to you would be the main problem for disincorporation. When you incorporate your business, you have gift relief and incorporation relief to avoid any CGT charge. Not so when you are transferring out of the company.

If there has been a substantial uplift in the value of property or goodwill, you could find the company is left with a large corporation tax charge on the capital gain.

Of course this will depend on the market value of the assets in the company.

You may see property and business/goodwill values reducing due to the current economic climate. In this case, now may be a good time to 'disincorporate' with a minimal tax capital gain.

Income tax

The other big problem with transferring your business into your own name is that there may well be an income tax charge on you personally. You and the company are treated as completely separate entities for tax purposes. As such, the company is essentially looked at in isolation. If the company transfers any assets to shareholders, the company would expect to receive proceeds worth the full value of that asset. If it does not, this will be classed as a distribution on the shareholders. Essentially, this is treated as a dividend receipt by the shareholders as they've extracted value from the company.

This treatment can apply whenever the company does not receive the full value from an asset transferred to shareholders.

Therefore, if you simply transferred goodwill from a company into your name not only would there be a disposal by the company, but you would be subject to income tax charge.

If you paid the company for the goodwill, it would only be the difference between the market value and the amount you paid that could be subject to income tax.

Example

Let us look at the example of Jack above. If he paid the company £400,000 for the goodwill, he would be classified as receiving a distribution of £100,000 from the company.

There is also a danger that any transfer of assets to director shareholders by the company could be subject to the 'benefit in kind' rules such that income tax and National Insurance Contributions could become payable.

Of course, if you did pay the company the full market value for any assets transferred to you, this would avoid any income tax charge.

The company would then hold the cash proceeds, and you would still have the problem of extracting the cash tax efficiently. Some options could include:

- Becoming non UK resident and extracting cash as a dividend free of income tax (subject to the temporary non-resident provisions)

- Extracting cash over the course of a number of tax years to utilise your basic rate tax band. This would allow cash to be extracted free of income tax

- You could simply use the cash in the company to undertake a new activity via the company (e.g., a new trade or investment business such as property development)

- The company could be wound up and the cash extracted as a capital distribution (and therefore subject to CGT at 28% or even less if Entrepreneurs Relief applies)

Other implications

Not only the CGT and potential income tax charge, there are other tax implications of transferring your business from your company into your own name.

Many of these apply as the company will be classed as ceasing to trade.

Here are some of the key ones to watch out for:

- You need to be very careful over the allocation of any trading losses in the company. These can in general only be offset against income of the company before it is wound up (although in some instances may be offset against trading profits of the preceding 36 months).

- Make sure that trading losses are utilised in the period before disincorporation as they will be lost after the trade has been transferred. For instance, any assets which may realise a capital gain should be sold before disincorporation if the company has made trading losses in the same accounting period.

Example

BBH Ltd had trading losses of £1M in the accounting period ended 31 December 2012 and £500,000 in the six months to 30 June 2013. It transferred its trade to the sole shareholder (Bill) on 30 June 2013.

It sold assets on 2 September 2013 which crystallised a capital gain of £400,000.

The trading losses in the company are effectively lost and cannot be offset against the capital gain of £400,000. If BBH had sold the assets on 2 June 2013 the £500,000 loss could have been offset against the gain and avoided a corporation tax charge.

Note that the losses will not even be carried forward as they are only carried forward in the company for offset against profits of the same trade (which is now no longer in the company).

- If there are any loans made to the directors, ensure these are re-paid to prevent a benefit in kind tax charge arising.

- Trading stock and debtors can generally be transferred free of tax.

Winding up the company and extracting the cash

Following the transfer of the trade, any surplus profits remaining within the company will need to be distributed to the shareholders.

There are main ways that you can extract cash from the company. Firstly, you could wind up the company and extract any cash as a capital distribution.

Alternatively, you could simply extract the cash as a dividend. The tax implications of both of these courses of action would depend crucially on your residence status.

Liquidate the company and pay a capital distribution.

If you are UK resident when you wind up the company, the advantage is that capital gains tax ('CGT') applies as opposed to income tax. The distribution of the cash to the shareholders would result in a gain for the shareholders, based on their ownership of the shares.

The key relief here will be Entrepreneurs relief.

Entrepreneurs Relief

This would tax the gain at a special 10% rate of CGT. The gain would arise on the amount received, less the amount paid/subscribed for the shares.

In order for the shares to qualify for Entrepreneurs relief, the company itself would need to be:

- A trading company of which you owned at least 5% of the shares
- Which you were an employee or officer of
- And which was owned by you, and actually traded for 12 months previously

Where these conditions apply, Entrepreneurs Relief can apply to the first £10,000,000 of any gain. The remaining gain is then taxed at 28%. Note that the £10,000,000 limit is a lifetime limit.

A further point to note is that the UK tax authorities take a narrow definition of trading and would not class a company as trading if it had any substantial non trading assets. "Substantial" in this context is usually taken to be in excess of 20% of net assets/income.

In the case of a company with a relatively high cash balance, the Revenue could regard this as substantial. The key issue would be to identify why the cash balance has arose and whether it is being accumulated for a business purposes. It may also be necessary to consider other similar companies in the sector to ascertain their cash levels.

Given the large impact Entrepreneurs Relief will have, it is essential to study the company's position in detail.

Therefore, a winding up could entitle you to a lower rate of CGT on the cash receipt. As shown above, whether the company will qualifies for Entrepreneurs Relief, the size of the gain and availability of the annual exemption would need to be considered.

Dividend extraction

The alternative would be to extract the cash as a dividend. You will suffer tax on the dividend at 25% if it's above the higher rate tax band (rising to 30.55% if above £150,000). If not you could receive it free of income tax.

For higher rate taxpayers, there will therefore be a substantial benefit in opting for the capital distribution treatment above.

This is not to say that capital treatment is always beneficial. If, for example, you had income tax losses, substantial tax credits (e.g., EIS income tax credits) were a basic rate taxpayer or were planning on leaving the UK, you may want to opt for a dividend.

Chapter 23

The Patent Box and the 10% Rate of Corporation Tax

As from 1 April 2013, the new Patent Box will be introduced.

This is a new tax regime for Intellectual Property ("IP") that reduces the corporation tax rate payable by UK companies on profits from qualifying IP.

The Patent Box is part of a package of tax changes intended by the UK Government to encourage multinationals to base their operations, in particular tech and innovation activities in the UK. Other countries such as the Netherlands, Luxembourg, Ireland or Switzerland have advantageous IP regimes. This will allow the UK to compete with these jurisdictions.

What is the Patent Box?

The Patent Box effectively applies a reduced UK corporation tax rate of 10% (the main rate being 23%, for 2013 reducing to 21% for 2014) to profits arising from 'qualifying IP rights' that are 'actively owned'.

The Patent Box will be introduced from 1 April 2013, with the full benefit being phased in over a 5 year period.

What IP qualifies for the Box?

Qualifying IP rights are broadly registered patents granted by the UK or European patent office, as well as certain other similar rights such as data exclusivity and plant variety rights.

It is also intended that the regime will apply to national patents of other EU member states to the extent such states have similar patent criteria as the UK.

Such patents can either be owned directly or by way of an exclusive license to exploit such patents in a designated national territory.

Importantly, for a patent to qualify, the company (or a member of the same group as the company) must have made a significant contribution to the development of the patent or an item that incorporates such patent. The Box will not apply to income derived from pre-developed patents that are acquired and then merely exploited.

Active ownership

The Box is not intended to apply to income derived from passive investment in IP. Qualifying patents must be actively owned, which broadly means that the company must be performing a significant amount of management activity in respect of the patent (e.g., maintaining protection, granting licences, and researching alternative applications).

What income falls in the Box?

The mechanism to calculate income that is subject to the 10% Patent Box rate is complex but broadly, and subject to certain adjustments, worldwide income from the following activities falls within the Box:

- sales of patented items or items incorporating patented items;
- licence fees and royalties from patented items;
- sales of patents;
- any infringement actions;
- deemed royalties for the internal use of a patent in activities that do not directly generate patent income (e.g., the use of a patent in the provision of services).

The Patent Box therefore has wide potential application - it is only necessary for one component of an item to be patented for the income derived from sales of the entire item to fall within the Box.

Chapter 24

When Non-resident Companies are Within the UK Corporation Tax Regime

Foreign businesses should be able to undertake significant UK activity without triggering tax liabilities.

Corporation Tax

The UK levies corporation tax on the world-wide income and chargeable gains of companies that are resident. As recently as 2008, the mainstream corporation tax rate was 30% but, in line with its policy of increasing the competitiveness of the UK, the coalition government has reduced the mainstream rate every year since coming to power.

A company incorporated in the UK will almost inevitably be tax resident there, but a foreign company which is "centrally managed and controlled" from the UK is also taxed as a UK resident.

The management and control test looks at the highest level of strategic control over a company's affairs. In the majority of cases this will be exercised by the Board of Directors in its formal meetings called to decide company policy. If those meetings take place in the UK the company will be UK resident, subject to the "tie-breaker article" under an applicable double tax treaty.

The location of a company's central management and control is a question of fact, and it may not always be exercised at Board meetings. For example, occasionally the usual functions of a Board may be carried out by some other committee or person such as a dominant director or a corporate managing agent, or the Board members may exercise their powers outside the formal Board meetings.

HMRC has explained its approach to this issue as follows:

- it first tries to ascertain whether the Board in fact exercises central management and control or whether it is exercised by some other person(s);

- if power does rest with the Board, HMRC seeks to determine where the directors exercise this central management and control (which is not necessarily where they meet); and

- in cases where the directors apparently do not exercise central management and control of the company, HMRC then looks to establish where and by whom it is exercised.

Biggest risk of being controlled from the UK?

Although any company incorporated outside the UK is subject to a theoretical risk of becoming UK tax resident under the central management and control test, that risk is greatest in relation to structured intermediaries which have a limited purpose within a corporate group or financing structure, so-called "special purpose vehicles" or "SPVs". SPVs are commonly established in low, or no tax jurisdictions with the intention, usually, to achieve tax neutrality and avoid "tax leakage" rather than to realise a positive tax advantage.

Although an SPV may undertake numerous transactions, perhaps regularly receiving and distributing payment streams, substantially all such transactions will be prescribed at the inception of the transaction or effected by a contractual counter-party under some form of asset management agreement.

A defining characteristic of such SPVs is that they do not usually initiate new transactions on their own account, and the ongoing involvement of the Board is potentially minimal which increases the risk that some other person may be viewed as controlling the company.

Where there is a risk, whether because of the composition of the Board, the delegation of management responsibilities or some other factor, that control of an offshore entity may be exercised from the UK. Tt is advisable to seek legal advice on the appropriate control and record keeping procedures necessary to create, and evidence, a factual defence against an HMRC challenge.

Permanent Establishment

For the majority of non-UK companies that begin to develop a UK customer-base, the most significant "tipping point" will concern the level of UK activity which is possible without going so far as to establish a taxable presence.

A non-UK company that maintains its control offshore may nevertheless become subject to UK corporation tax if it begins to carry on any part of its trade through a UK "permanent establishment". In that case, subject to the terms of an applicable double tax treaty, tax will be charged on its UK profits or, more likely, the profits it would have earned from its UK activity had all it business been undertaken on an arm's length basis in compliance with the UK's transfer pricing rules.

A "permanent establishment" usually means a branch office or other fixed place of business, in which case there is seldom much doubt as to whether one has been established. However, a taxable presence may also be established simply by engaging one or more dependent agents who have the authority to conclude contracts on behalf of the foreign company and who regularly do so with customers in the UK.

At first sight this might suggest that a company will be liable for corporation tax immediately if it puts employees or representatives "on the ground" in the UK. But, not every form of business activity performed in the UK, whether through a branch or a dependent agent, will trigger corporation tax liabilities.

A company that may be considering engaging UK-based personnel for the first time or even establishing a UK office on a speculative basis may be able to arrange its preliminary steps so as to delay the point at which tax registration, reporting and payment obligations may arise.

Whilst a company is merely testing the UK demand for its products or services, it may be possible to restrict the activity of its UK personnel so as to avoid crossing the trading threshold. So, for example, if the role of the agents is limited to marketing, so that any contracts being entered into are either on standard terms or executed outside the UK by the company rather than on its behalf by the UK agent. It should be possible to avoid trading at least until it becomes clear that there is a viable market for the company in the UK. Similarly, if the activities of the branch are limited to publicity, research and customer support, making it, in effect, a "representative office", actual trading and, consequently, UK corporation tax may be avoided.

Careful structuring to avoid having a permanent establishment can lead to significant tax savings. For instance, it has been stated that despite having UK sales in excess of £3.3 billion, Amazon pays no UK corporation tax because it carries on only an "order fulfillment" business in the UK with a Luxembourg entity being the legal supplier of goods.

Chapter 25

Trading in the UK with a UK company or LLP

If you are a non UK resident looking to carry out any business activities in the UK, you should carefully consider whether there could be a charge to UK tax, and if so, how this can be mitigated.

As we have seen in the previous chapter as a non UK resident you are generally outside the scope of UK tax provided you aren't engaged in a UK trade via a UK permanent establishment.

One of the two circumstances in which there can be a permanent establishment is where there is a fixed place of business in the UK through which the trade is carried on.

Agency

The other occasion when there can be a permanent establishment is via a UK dependent agent.

The tax legislation treats the following as a permanent establishment:

'...an agent acting on behalf of the company where the agent has and habitually exercises authority to do business on behalf of the company. Such is true, as long as that agent is not of independent status acting in the ordinary course of his business."

If you have someone in the UK acting on your behalf who isable to enter into contracts on your behalf (i.e., binding you as the offshore principal), that person would represent a permanent establishment and lead the way for you to be taxed on the UK profits.

You would need to ensure that you had no UK agent.

Using an offshore company

The best option if you are non-resident may be to use a non UK resident company. This would completely avoid UK corporation tax and also reduce any UK disclosure.

You could consider a company in the Isle of Man which offers 0% corporation tax and can also obtain an EU VAT number.

If you are non-resident, there would be no issues in terms of the company being UK resident and if there is no UK permanent establishment there would be no UK corporation tax on the profits. In addition, if the receipts are not royalties they would not be subject to UK withholding tax. Receipts could be payable into either a UK or IOM bank account and based on the assumptions above there should be no UK tax due.

Double tax treaties would not be an issue with an offshore company as there is unlikely to be a treaty in place. Note that there is a limited treaty between the UK and IOM which effectively provides that profits in the UK would be taxable to the extent there is a permanent establishment. This is therefore similar to the UK's s domestic provisions.

If using an offshore company were not an option, and you wanted to use a UK entity, you could use either a UK company or a UK limited liability partnership.

UK company

If using a UK company, it would be charged to UK corporation tax on its worldwide income and gains. The most effective option would be to use the UK company as an agency company contracting with the clients but not being classed as an agent for the definition of the permanent establishment provisions (e.g. no power to bind the offshore principal/independent agent and no UK fixed place of business).

The receipts would be taken via the UK company and would be paid to you or another offshore entity, less a small commission (e.g., 5%). The commission rate would need to be set at a market rate and the income of the company would be the 5% received. It could then offset any expenses before corporation tax was applied.

The UK company would not be taxed on the entire income it received on behalf of an offshore principal, but it would clearly be taxed on its commission receipts.

The downside is that UK accounts and an annual return would need to be filed along with corporation tax returns. Shareholders and Directors details would need to be disclosed to the UK tax authorities.

UK reporting

In terms of the accounts for the UK company, it would be essential to determine whether for accounting purposes it acted as principal or agent.

UK reporting standards state that in order for a company to be viewed as a principal, it should normally have exposure to all significant benefits and risks associated with at least one of the following:

(a) Selling price: the ability, within economic constraints, to establish the selling price with the customer, either directly or, where the selling price of an item is fixed, indirectly by providing additional goods or services or adjusting the terms of a linked transaction; or

(b) Stock: exposure to the risks of damage, slow movement and obsolescence, and changes in suppliers' prices.

Where the seller has not disclosed that it is acting as agent, there is a rebuttable presumption that it is acting as principal.

Additional factors which indicate that a seller may be acting as principal include:

(a) performance of part of the services, or modification to the goods supplied;

(b) assumption of credit risk; and

(c) discretion in supplier selection.

By contrast where a seller acts as agent, it will not normally be exposed to the majority of the benefits and risks associated with the transaction. Agency arrangements will typically include the following characteristics:

(a) the seller has disclosed the fact that it is acting as agent;

(b) once the seller has confirmed its customer's order with a third party, the seller will normally have no further involvement in the performance of the ultimate supplier's contractual obligations;

(c) the amount that the seller earns is predetermined, being either a fixed fee per transaction or a stated percentage of the amount billed to the customer; and

(d) the seller bears no stock or credit risk, other than in circumstances where it receives additional consideration from the ultimate supplier in return for its assumption of this risk.

Where the substance of a transaction is that the company acts as agent, it should report as turnover in the accounts for the commission received in return for its performance under the agency arrangement.

Any amounts received that are payable to the offshore principal would not be included in the agent's turnover.

You would therefore need to determine whether the UK company could be classed as an agent for the purposes of the accounts. Look at the substance of the transaction. If there is no disclosure of the principal, there is a rebuttable presumption that the UK company would be the principal - and would therefore, report all the turnover and the subsequent payments back to the offshore company.

Limited Liability Partnership ('LLP')

The alternative option would be to use an LLP. This is a pass through entity for UK tax purposes and therefore the income would be attributed to you personally. Providing the profits are not profits of a UK trade and you are non UK resident, there would be no UK income tax charge on the profits.

This therefore has an advantage over the UK Ltd company above in that it can avoid all UK tax.

In terms of disclosure, the notes to the Partnership return specifically state that '...Where all the partners are not resident in the UK, the Partnership Tax Return should enter only the profits arising from UK operations...'. Therefore if the partnership had no UK trading profit the partnership return would effectively be blank.

The downside of an LLP is that it would need to file accounts with companies house showing its profit and loss account and balance sheet, even though it may conduct its business entirely overseas.

Chapter 26

Liquidating companies in 2013

The tax treatment of company distributions on a winding up have changed significantly from 1 March 2012. In this chapter, we look at how the new rules operate and any tax planning opportunities available.

Old Rules

Under the "old rules" (ESC C16), it was possible for a distribution to be made on a company wind up and to be taxed as a capital receipt in the hands of the shareholder.

In many cases, capital treatment is preferred to income treatment as it means that CGT is payable at 28% (if a higher rate taxpayer) or 10% (if Entrepreneurs Relief is available).

If it were not classed as a capital distribution, it would be taxed as a dividend at either 25% or 30.55% if the shareholders income was above the historic higher rate band.

New rules

New legislation has been introduced which states that a distribution made on or after 1 March 2012 will be taxed as a capital receipt where the following conditions are satisfied:

- the distribution must have been made by the company in anticipation of the company's winding up
- the company must have secured, or must have intended to secure, the payment of any sums due to it;
- the company must have satisfied, or must have intended to satisfy, any debts or liabilities; and

- the amount of the distribution (or the total of that distribution and any earlier "relevant" distributions) must not exceed the cap of £25,000.

Capital treatment will be withdrawn if the company has not been dissolved and has either: (1) failed to satisfy all of its debts and liabilities; or (2) failed to secure all payments due to it, within two years.

So the big change is that capital treatment will only apply on the winding up (as opposed to a full liquidation) if the extraction is less than £25,000.

Applying the cap

Now that we have a cap, we must apply it. There are three important points to note here:

(1)the cap applies by reference to the distributions made by the company and not to the distributions received by a shareholder (although it is the shareholder that will feel the effect of the legislation). The cap will be breached if the total relevant distributions made by the company exceed £25,000. This is the case regardless of whether or not the amount received by the recipient exceeds £25,000;

(2)any earlier relevant distributions must be taken into account in determining if a relevant distribution breaches the cap. Remember that any distributions made when the company 'intends' to wind up are relevant distributions.

(3)the cap applies on an all or nothing basis. If a relevant distribution exceeds £25,000 then all of that distribution will be taxed as income in the hands of the shareholder, not just the excess amount.

There are a number of potential problems here not least how to determine if a distribution is a relevant distribution. At what point does a company intend to wind up? There will also be compliance issues in some cases such as where a dividend is received by a minority shareholder in a company in which he or she has had little involvement. Will that shareholder be in a position to know the total amount of relevant distributions made by the company?

Planning points

Here are some of the key planning points:

- Firstly capital treatment may not necessarily be preferred. Where the amount of the distribution is only within the shareholders basic rate band, an income distribution would be preferred anyway (as this would be tax free).

- The cap only applies to distributions on a winding up. You can still secure capital treatment for larger distributions if you opt for a full liquidation. Of course, the downside will be the increased cost, but where larger amounts are extracted the income tax savings could easily cover this.

- There are other opportunities to extract capital distributions, most notably where the company has a large share capital and you reduce that share capital. This would be paid to the shareholder and taxed as a capital distribution. The £25,000 cap would not apply to this and therefore, capital treatment for amounts larger than £25,000 could be obtained.

- Although the cap is "all or nothing", if the amount to be extracted is larger than this, it could be attractive to pay an income distribution while the company is still trading, and then extract the remaining cash (less than £25,000) when the company is being wound up. Remember that the income dividend would need to be paid before the company had an intention to be wound up.

Pay Less Tax!

... with help from www.WealthProtectionReport.co.uk

- **Tax Planning Techniques Of The Rich & Famous** - Essential reading for anyone who wants to use the same tax planning techniques as the most successful Entrepreneurs, large corporations and celebrities

- **Tax Planning For Company Owners** – Tells you everything you need to know to minimise both personal and corporate taxes if you use a UK Limited Company

- **Using Offshore Companies – The Complete Tax Guide** – Detailed analysis of when and how you can use offshore companies to reduce your UK taxes

- **Using Offshore Trusts – The A-Z Guide** – Detailed analysis of when and how you can use offshore trusts to reduce your UK taxes

- **Asset Protection Handbook –** Looks at strategies to ringfence your assets in today's increasing litigious climate

- **Tax Planning For The Statutory Residence Test In 2013 –** Detailed information on how the new Statutory Residence Test applies and how to take advantage of the rules to reduce UK tax

- **Offshore Tax Secrets 2013** – Top ways to use offshore strategies to reduce your UK taxes

- **Tax Saving Tactics For Non Doms** – Essential reading for all non UK domiciliaries

- **The Worlds Best Tax Havens** – Detailed analysis of the tax and residency requirements for over 20 of the worlds best tax havens

9206447R00069

Printed in Great Britain
by Amazon.co.uk, Ltd.,
Marston Gate.